BECOMING KATHRINE TALBOT

This is the true story of the author Kathrine Talbot. It is based on her letters, diaries, and autobiographical accounts, on interviews with witnesses, and on historical documents. Her biographer takes responsibility for any factual errors. And he knows that his protagonist wasn't particularly fond of biographies.

Becoming Kathrine Talbot

A JEWISH REFUGEE AND
THE NOVELIST SHE INVENTED

Christoph Ribbat

VALLENTINE MITCHELL
LONDON • CHICAGO

First published in 2024 by Vallentine Mitchell

Catalyst House,
720 Centennial Court,
Centennial Park, Elstree WD6 3SY, UK

814 N. Franklin Street,
Chicago, Illinois,
IL 60610 USA

www.vmbooks.com

British Library Cataloguing in Publication Data:
An entry can be found on request

ISBN 978 1 80371 061 7 (PB)
ISBN 978 1 80371 062 4 (EB)
ISBN 978 1 80371 063 1 (Kindle)

Library of Congress Cataloging in Publication Data:
An entry can be found on request

Contents

1

Stones

The maid is nineteen years old; she dreams of being a poet. They deport her on a Monday morning. She's doing the laundry when the policeman arrives. It is an especially warm day in May, and she's just been looking out the window thinking that the clothes are going to dry very quickly in this kind of weather. She's not an excellent maid. Household matters leave her cold. But this much she knows.

There's a rumor going around in this country. People say young women like her might send secret signals to the pilots of enemy planes: by choosing specific patterns in which they hang trousers, shirts, and sheets on outdoor laundry lines. That's one reason to lock maids up in camps.[1]

The policeman has brought his wife along. She says that if she were at home, she would also be doing the laundry. Instead, she is helping with the deportation process. The policeman's wife tells the maid to pack warm clothes, too, despite the wonderful weather, just in case. That doesn't sound good.

In her room, the maid looks for clothes for spring, summer, autumn, and winter. If her parents were here, they would expect her to be courageous and stay calm. The policeman's wife is watching her. The maid folds things. She makes piles. She puts the piles into her suitcase. Looking up, she notices the tears in the other woman's eyes.

* * * * *

Twelve years later, the maid, no longer a maid, will publish her first novel. She will write in the language she's only learning now. Three years after her debut, her second novel will come out, and four years after that, her third book. The international press will praise her work and some critics will point out weak spots. She will not be read all over the world, but on two sides of an ocean. A highly influential newspaper will call her a "natural novelist."

They take the maid to prison, in the nearest town. She's part of a group of about fifty female inmates. All of them were deported from nearby towns and villages.

The maid fled to this country just one and a half years ago. She used forged papers. More than six hundred miles south of here, a gentleman behind a desk told her that he had an idea, and another gentleman produced documents for her. On a form, the man filled in the name of a school she was going to attend. She never went to that school, of course, and she never will. Her parents also tried to escape, legally, and at first it seemed to work out for them, but then it didn't. She has a sister whom she has never met, and never will. She's seen a lock of her hair, though.

After two days in prison, they take her and the others to a train station. More deported women join them, hundreds of them, of all ages. Some have little children. They all get onto a train that moves, stops, creeps along, stops again. Then it stands still, for hours on end. It's hot. The women and the children are thirsty, hungry, and afraid. Babies cry. Then they sleep and then they cry again. One woman in her train carriage has six sons. All six of them are soldiers. They are all fighting for the country that will now imprison their mother. The government is deporting scientists, musicians, sculptors, nurses, many maids, some nuns, and a lot of housewives.

Now the train starts moving again. They reach the station of a big city. They are led away from the station. Buses are parked here. The women and children get on the buses, the doors close, the buses move through the city. The maid looks out the window. There are people standing by the side of the street and they seem to have been waiting for them. They throw stones at the buses. Some people who really wanted to throw something evidently couldn't find stones, so they throw clumps of earth instead. They appear to despise the women and children on the buses: people like her.

The buses take the detainees to warehouses by the docks. It seems as if these buildings have stood empty for some time. They're dirty and dusty inside. There are six toilets between hundreds of women. Soon the toilets are clogged up. Nobody's thought of the fact that some of the deported women might be menstruating. Nobody tells them what's going to happen next.

* * * * *

Whereas in prison, they had straw mattresses, here, there's just the bare wooden floor. At night the maid lies awake. She watches what's going on.

Women get up to walk around. She hears murmurs and screams. In the dark she makes a vow: One day she will write about these experiences. But it's going to be difficult to keep her promise. For a very long time she won't be able to tell anyone about what she's experiencing now, nor about what she endured before she escaped to this country, nor about the unimaginable things happening to her parents and her sister. Her name is Ilse Gross. Her novels will appear under the name Kathrine Talbot. There will come a time when she'll finally be able to tell this story. But that time will almost come too late.

In the morning, some ladies arrive. They belong to a benefit organization. They bring sweetened tea. Twice a day there's thin stew and, per person, two slices of white bread spread with margarine. After the third night, the women are once again taken to buses. Are people going to throw stones again? The buses start moving. The entire world is going to love this city one day, for fantastic musicians with trend-setting haircuts. The maid will never quite forgive Liverpool and its people.

The ride only takes two minutes. No stones are thrown. The maid is hungry. She feels dirty. They're still at the harbor. The bus doors open. The maid and all the other women board a ship.

And then the ship leaves the harbor for the open seas and after a while a bell rings. None of the women know what that means. So they don't react. They just stay where they are. Sometime later, one of the crew members appears and leads them inside. There are paper bags on long tables and every one of the women is supposed to take one of them. They hold the bags. They open them and look inside. Once they realize what the bags contain, many of the women break down in tears.

2

English

Ilse Gross grew up in Bingen, Germany. There the River Nahe flows into the River Rhine, Klopp Castle sits on Klopp Mountain, and the Mouse Tower stands on Mouse Tower Island. She's the daughter of a wine merchant. She spent her Bingen childhood with her mother, father, uncles, aunts, and cousins. Happy times. Until Ilse broke down. One day, when she was fourteen, she came home from school, threw herself on her bed, started crying and didn't stop.

Three wine regions meet in Bingen: Rheinhessen, Nahe, and Rheingau. In the 1930s, Ilse's hometown called itself "The Happy Wine Town on the Rhine." When ships were going up the river towards Bingen they passed the famous Loreley rock. In that moment passengers would start singing that old song about the siren combing her golden hair on that exact spot. Some of the dreamier tourists still sang the song when it was clear to everyone that Heinrich Heine, the Jewish poet, was now banned, and that the song based on his poem was deemed unsingable.

On the banks of the Rhine, Bingen's visitors got a pretzel at "Bretzelbub." They bought postcards at a kiosk. One motif on the card carousels appeared in a number of different variations: the dictator. Here he was: with a dog, with children, in uniform, in a trench coat, in a tailcoat, in a morning suit. The visitors then had a glass of wine or two. According to the local paper, inebriated tourists and their troublesome urinating habits were a problem in Bingen. In a tent by the Rhine, a band played dance music seven days a week. "Annemarie" was one of their standards. "And if a bullet shoots me dead / Well, then I won't come back / Don't cry until your eyes are red / Just take another chap." Drunken Bingen visitors sang "Annemarie" when they were staggering through the town's quaint streets. The Rhine, a local brochure said, was the "River of German Fate." Hours spent on its shore were "hours of deep experience."[1]

A brief walk away from the Rhine, in the Gross family apartment, atop the wine business on the lower floors of the building, Ilse wouldn't stop crying. Her parents asked their daughter questions. She just cried. Eventually they called Dr. Mehler. He climbed up the stairs. He examined Ilse.

Her new math teacher had moved Ilse and the five other Jewish students in her class to the back row of the classroom. She had told them never to speak a word in class again. Then she had given a lecture about the Jews as a "lower life form." And she had encouraged the "Aryan" students to make life as hard as possible for these six girls. For two more days, Ilse had still managed to go to school, until she couldn't do it anymore.

Concluding his visit, Dr. Mehler had no specific recommendations. Ilse stayed home for a few more weeks. Then she left the Happy Wine Town for Switzerland. She was all by herself, and she was fourteen years old. It was her first escape from Bingen.

* * * * *

In November 1938, three years later, seventeen-year-old Ilse Eva Gross boards a plane in Zurich. She's headed for Croydon, London's international airport. The plane takes off and sets a course for the country that will deport her eighteen months later – as an "enemy alien."

She had expected to take the train through France. But she didn't get the papers she needed. Then her parents, and probably also friends of her parents, came up with the money for her flight. She's never been on a plane before.

First the channel appears below her, and then England. Ilse's mother and father still live in Bingen. That seems horrible now. Her parents are both Jews. They haven't left Germany yet because they want to protect Ilse's sister. Her sister needs protection. Just a few days before her departure, Ilse heard reports on the radio about burning synagogues.

Because she's spent the last few years in Geneva, her French is excellent. Her third language: very poor English. She was a student at Geneva's International School. Some of her fellow students were American and she really could have learned English from them. But they impressed her too much. They were so confident and so good-looking, laid-back and impeccably dressed. This one boy knew everything about politics, and in addition, as if it were nothing, he played the piano unbelievably well. Chopin. She heard Chopin so often in Geneva. But she admired this boy only from afar.

And then she sees the airport. The plane circles over South London, and she looks out the window and at that very moment the lights go on in Croydon. Somebody told her before she left that there was a surplus of women in England. Ilse doesn't think of herself as particularly attractive. She's convinced she won't ever find a boyfriend in this country. But that's not what's on her mind right now. She thinks of her parents. She's the one-person advance party in her family's escape. Her father and mother, too, will have to leave Germany. Maybe they'll come to England. Maybe they'll make it directly to the United States.

✶ ✶ ✶ ✶ ✶

After landing in Croydon, she arrives in another London suburb. Her cousin Willy, his wife, and their son live in a small red-brick house in a very long row of other small red-brick houses. Ilse walks in the front door, takes a few steps, and already she is standing by the back door.

More than thirty years older than Ilse, Willy's more of an uncle than a cousin. In Heidelberg he lived in a mansion. Here in London, she sees German furniture, heavy oak, elegant maple, and realizes that in Heidelberg there was a lot more room around these pieces.

The radio's tuned to the BBC. "In Town Tonight." She looks at the table in front of her and at a waxed tablecloth. Her cousin and she both come from a world where tables are always covered with textile. Her maternal grandfather's company produced innovative new tablecloths whose colors wouldn't run in the wash – a flourishing business before the Nazi years. Now Ilse looks at this semi-tasteful waxed covering, black with red dots, and it suddenly becomes clear to her that she has never set foot in a household as modest as this one. Which probably means that everything in her life has changed.

✶ ✶ ✶ ✶ ✶

If she could have stayed in Geneva, she would have gone to a school for aspiring librarians. She owned a pair of silver dancing shoes. She could have kept going dancing, meeting friends, taking walks along the lake. But her parents couldn't afford her life in Geneva anymore. And her Swiss residency permit was about to expire.

Like many young people in those years, she had put up a picture of "The Unknown Woman of the Seine" on her bedroom wall. It portrayed an attractive Parisian found dead in the water. When it was completely unclear what would happen to Ilse – it was impossible to go back to Germany and just as impossible to remain in Switzerland – she was standing at the lake and looking at the swans of Geneva, and she imagined ending her life like the most popular drowned woman of her era. Something about that felt romantic. And then she held a visa for the United Kingdom.

✳ ✳ ✳ ✳ ✳

Tens of thousands of people march through English streets in the 1930s. Their hands shoot up to form the infamous salute. And they sing Nazi songs in English translation. These crowds belong to the antisemitic "British Union of Fascists."[2] But counter demonstrators block their way. And in churches, synagogues, and unions, initiatives form, demanding more generous refugee policies for the persecuted German Jews. Across the country, Britons give money to the "Movement for the Care of Children from Germany."[3]

After the Night of Broken Glass in November 1938, the House of Commons decides to let ten thousand Jewish children and youth enter the United Kingdom – on a non-permanent basis. Though the parents of these young people are also in danger, they will not receive visas. There's extensive unemployment and an economic crisis, and common sense seems to dictate that you simply can't find room for everyone. There's only the Kindertransport. Or at least the Kindertransport.

In Germany, Poland, Austria and Czechoslovakia, fathers and mothers take their children to train stations. Some of these parents hold their children tightly and kiss them again and again. It could be the last time, after all. Others use tenderness sparingly. They want to make it seem as though everyone's going to see each other again very, very soon. The father of one girl kneels before her, on the station platform, and pleads with her to do everything she can to get her parents, her grandparents, her aunt, and her cousins out of Austria and into England. The girl is ten years old.[4] The parents wave as the daughters and sons leave the station.

The fate of most of the people left behind will defy human imagination. The trains cross Germany and the Netherlands, the children board ferries, and when these reach England, the children, their identity tags around their necks, wave for the press. Photographers take pictures of girls rather than boys. Male refugees aren't as popular with readers. The first English meal these children eat – stew – is also documented in pictures. At Liverpool Street Station, families pick them up. Or they find homes in institutions.

To some, the Kindertransport will serve as a testament to British generosity. It's heart-warming that so many people are willing to take in young refugees and treat them like their own children. Other observers will see the Kindertransport as emblematic of a flawed refugee policy. Most of the parents of the saved children will fall victim to murderous German antisemitism. Even in November 1938, the severe danger they're in is plain to see. No other British salvation measure will be as extensively documented as the Kindertransport; none other will be discussed with such controversy.[5]

* * * * *

Bertha, Ilse's sister, fifteen years older than she, has severe mental and bodily handicaps. Her brain was damaged during birth. For as long as Ilse can remember, Bertha has been living in a home, thirty miles down the Rhine from Bingen.

When she was a child, Ilse drew pictures for Bertha and her parents took the pictures to Bertha's home. Ilse wrote poems about her sister. She cultivated a kind of romantic obsession with her. Sitting at the piano, she improvised musical pieces for her, pieces that Bertha never got to hear. Ilse kept that lock of Bertha's hair, beautiful and brown. She often asked her parents to take her along to see her. The parents always said they'd rather spare Ilse. It's not a taboo subject, they do discuss Bertha, but it was definitive that Ilse wasn't supposed to ever meet her. Before Christmas, Ilse's mother assembled care packages for Bertha and the home's staff. She sent nighties, slippers, soap, boxes of biscuits. Bertha learned to write when she was twenty-four years old. Ilse received a postcard from her: a few capital letters written on the card with obvious effort. At some point Ilse's romantic affection for Bertha evaporated, and along with it, her wish to see her.

Since 1933, many people around Ilse's parents have left Bingen and Germany: Jewish neighbors, friends, relatives. Karl and Agnes Gross have stayed on, because of Bertha. Even early in the Nazi Era, people know that the new system targets the disabled. A 1938 poster shows a man with a "hereditary disease" and indicates that this man cost the "Volksgemeinschaft" 60,000 Reichsmark. While the placard only hints at practical consequences, German bureaucrats and physicians are already working on exterminatory plans.[6]

* * * * *

The United Kingdom saves another group of refugees. It's twice as large as the one rescued by the Kindertransport. 20,000 Jewish women from Germany, Austria, and Poland escape Nazi terror by becoming British maids. If you commit to working as a domestic, you receive a British visa. But these women don't arrive as a group. No photographers wait for them. There's no stew. One by one they disappear into the households in which they cook, serve and clean. Most of them haven't worked as maids before. Some of them only know how to keep maids busy.

It isn't sheer altruism that motivates this program. There's a servant crisis in 1930s Britain and the government aims for the refugee women to ameliorate it. British working-class girls don't want to work as maids anymore. It's terrible: the affluent just can't find help. Maybe it's because many employers don't let maids use long-handled mops. Tradition demands that maids kneel on the floor while scrubbing. Young women will also realize that in sexual harassment cases, the guilty party is almost always quickly found: the maid herself. In addition, maids are generally not allowed to use their employers' bathrooms. What they get is a chamber pot, reminding them in the most intimate way of their exclusion from the family they live with and work for.[7]

* * * * *

Ilse is sitting next to a bathtub. She tells stories to a child soaking in the water. She has moved out of Cousin Willy's bungalow. Now she's a maid, albeit unpaid. Officially she's a student. That's what her fraudulent visa says. The seven-year-old English girl in the bath corrects the grammatical errors in Ilse's stories.

Ilse doesn't have to clean on her knees. Every night, for an hour, her mistress reads scenes from Shakespeare plays to her daughter and her maid. The mother thinks her daughter's a genius. She's less impressed by Ilse's abilities. Ilse sits on one cushion, the girl sits on another cushion, the mistress sits in an armchair, next to the lamp. To Ilse, listening feels like exercising on a trapeze. She's flying from one English word she understands to the next familiar-sounding one. Often there's a lot of air between these words.

When her mistress leaves Shakespeare behind, the time of *The Wouldbegoods* begins: six best friends, English children, Oswald, Dora, Dicky, Alice, Noël, and H.O. One summer long, the Wouldbegoods experience adventures in the countryside. Far from the city, Ilse's employer reads, people are friendlier, simply because there are fewer of them. Hence there's more friendliness per person, like a pound of butter that can be spread more generously on one loaf of bread than on several loaves.[8]

Ilse's always hungry. There's no bread in this house. There's porridge for breakfast. That's the most substantial meal. For lunch, early in the week, she gets a little piece of the Sunday roast on her plate. On Thursdays: maybe a small sausage. What she'll get later in the week remains to be seen. There's a biscuit in the afternoon. In the evening she learns what a "water biscuit" tastes like, and Bovril. A scraping of Bovril. Her haggard employer never seems to eat. Her daughter gets eggs and apples. But not the maid.

When the cleaning lady comes, she brings some bread for Ilse. They dust and talk. The cleaning lady tells her that her husband beats her and how happy she is when he's not at home. Clearly she finds Ilse and her elegant dresses interesting and strange and she says that the way Ilse talks reminds her of a Welsh accent. Ilse has no idea what a Welsh accent sounds like. Nor does she know what or where Wales is. She is grateful for the bread. She knows the cleaning lady can't really afford to help her out.

People say you should speak English as if you had a plum in your mouth. Hungry Ilse lies awake at nights. In Bingen, when they had company, beef bouillon, the colour of gold, was served first, and in the bouillon, you saw little islands of bone marrow dumplings. Warm rolls sat beneath cloth napkins in silver baskets. Then there was a roast, vegetables, salad, and, for dessert, home-made ice cream, maybe even a "bombe," and then fruit and cheese.

Hungry Ilse gets up to look out the window. From here she can see a grand house close by. She watches the servants there preparing the trays for what will surely be an opulent breakfast in the morning. Hungry Ilse goes back to bed and dreams of Swiss chocolate, German comfort food, restaurant buffets. She imagines how the rich family will invite her over. How they will offer her cake, how she will move into one of their elegant rooms. How these rich people will adopt her soon after, and how finally, after her new family have moved heaven and earth, her parents' plane will touch down in Croydon and, crying tears of joy, they'll all fall into each other's arms.

* * * * *

Once before the war, in 1935, she'd visited London with her mother. They went to see distant relatives. Mother Gross and daughter Gross told stories and their hosts listened. The public swimming baths in Bingen were now closed to Jews, they recounted. In a hamlet close-by, a sign said: "The street to Jerusalem does not lead through this village." And a Hitler Youth had thrown a stone at Ilse. When mother and daughter were done with their accounts, the London relatives weighed in. They were quite certain that all of this would go back to normal very soon. It couldn't be all that bad. Stiff upper lip. Very British. And Ilse wanted these relatives to like her. So she said that it hadn't really been a stone that hit her. More of a pebble, which had certainly struck her head, but hadn't injured her much.

Only later did she realize that this London trip hadn't been planned as a tourist adventure. Her parents had wanted Ilse to stir up compassion. They had hoped that the relatives would take Ilse in, so that one of the Gross daughters would be safe. Without success. And not long after their return from London, another stone came flying, no pebble this time, through the windowpane of the family's parlor. It hit the armchair the father was so fond of sitting in. At that moment, it was empty.

* * * * *

The mistress of the house can't stand Ilse's clumsiness. She herself hates housework and has an ugly temper. She's a theosophist. Everything the universe contains, individuals hold within them, in latent form. Ilse's employer most likely believes in this theosophic principle.

But what is latent within this maid? Ilse Gross has extensive knowledge of the oeuvre of French playwright Jean Giraudoux, loves Dostoevsky's *The Brothers Karamazov,* and has considerable expertise in Strindberg's plays. In 1937 she won third prize in the literature contest for the German-speaking students at International School Geneva, for "Snapshots of our Everyday Life," a poem composed in a rather complex rhyme scheme. She has taken courses in double-entry bookkeeping and in French business correspondence, in typing and in modern multilingual stenography.

Now Ilse pushes the vacuum cleaner through the flat. To operate such an instrument is a luxurious privilege for an English maid. Her whole life long, Ilse will keep the secret that she attended a Swiss housekeeping school in the summer of 1936, under the direction of one Mme. Dr. Rittmeyer. Maybe she didn't apply herself much back then. Here in London, the seven-year-old's socks disappear into the vacuum cleaner. Then the machine sucks up one of her mistress's stockings and stops working. The theosophist does have a temper.

✳ ✳ ✳ ✳ ✳

From Bingen, her parents try to help. The situation must change. Ilse can't be hungry all the time. They want her to visit a London friend of the family, a former customer of Gross and Sons. Bingen wines are esteemed in England. The Riesling is fantastic – that's a known fact, even over here. Ilse puts on something sophisticated and takes off for her appointment. The gentleman lives on Regent's Park, in an elegant, spacious flat. He sits behinds his desk and listens to the stories of Ilse's sufferings and her parent's worries. It is terrifying to think that they're still in Germany, and it is so urgent for them to get out. The family's friend has an idea. He is very willing to help. As he regularly receives first night theater tickets, for the London stages, from now on he will send Ilse these tickets. Free of charge.

✳ ✳ ✳ ✳ ✳

A German-Jewish medical student, now a refugee maid in England, serves dog biscuits to human beings at a party thrown by her employees. It was an honest mistake. She gets fired.

Another maid, twenty-one years old, must eat in the kitchen by herself. No maid ever eats in the family's dining room. She's dead tired. In a household of six people, she's the only servant. She should feel happy to be safe from antisemitic persecution. She should be grateful because life is so indescribably worse over there. But that doesn't keep her from crying. The family dog sitting next to her starts to lick the tears from her face.

A maid named Edith, who escaped from Berlin, has an English mistress who's also called Edith. From now on, the Edith in charge will call the other Edith Mary.[9] And there's an Austrian concert pianist who is now a servant and who has her employers' permission to touch the piano in the family sitting room. But they remind her to only ever play when she's sure that there's no one at home.

In the British class system, these new maids don't really fit in. Servants aren't supposed to have talents beyond those needed for household work. Their employers don't want to be told about the terrible developments on the Continent. They certainly don't want to hear about whatever worked better over there, before 1933, as compared to the British Isles. And employers are always right. Without their letter of recommendation, you'll never find another job.[10]

✶ ✶ ✶ ✶ ✶

Ilse uses the tickets the gentleman from Regent's Park sends her. She goes to see *The Flashing Stream* at the Lyric Theatre in Soho. An excellent male mathematician and an excellent female mathematician collaborate on a remote, though British, island. They develop new cruise missiles. But they're having trouble focusing on mathematical problems.[11]

Ilse invites her mistress to the theater. Her mistress rushes off to buy a new dress for the occasion. It is made of bright blue taffeta. Ilse doesn't need to shop. She owns enough fancy dresses.

Then Ilse is fired. She finds refuge in Cousin Willy's cramped little house. He's sitting at the kitchen table with his colleagues, all German refugees. They're studying for the British exam that could turn them back into recognized scientists. Somehow all these medical terms, terms they've been using in German for decades, will have to re-enter their heads in English. Willy was a psychiatry professor at the University of Heidelberg. He's the author of an important study about the psychology of extreme happiness. His work distinguishes between "happiness affect," which covers all other psychic processes, and "happiness inebriation," which pushes everything else from one's consciousness.[12]

Cousin Willy tells Ilse that she has to change her behavior. Being humble and disciplined is now all-important. Maybe the theosophist will give her another chance. Willy reminds her to think of her parents, still in Bingen. To think how happy she should feel to even be here.

There's plenty of reading material that might help you to cope in England. There's *Mistress and Maid*. Or: *While You Are in England*. Or: *Do's and Don'ts for Refugees*. In English homes, the booklets say, it's often quite a bit colder than in Continental ones. Wear warm underwear or wool coats indoors. Read English books. Don't listen to rumors. "Authentic information" is only supplied by newspapers and the radio. Always be "cheerful." Show a "smiling face." That's how you make friends. The English mistress will request something she needs. But this request isn't really a request. It is an order and must be followed instantly. Talk softly and walk softly, whether at home or in the streets. Don't dress extravagantly. Don't behave extravagantly. Choose understatement over overstatement. Speak English, always English. Bad English is preferable to any other language.[13]

And Ilse does get a second chance with the theosophist. She chooses overstatement over understatement to tell her how great life was in Bingen on the Rhine before 1933. She scatters her extravagant clothes all over her room. She doesn't have any trouble speaking bad English. But her clumsiness hasn't gone away. There comes a point when even Cousin Willy can no longer help her.

She takes the train to Stoke-on-Trent. In the home of her new employers, she lives below stairs. She's not supposed to ever speak to the father of the family. After just one week, she takes the train back to London.

She is lucky and finds a new job. In a south London suburb, she works for three affluent women who live together. There's always enough to eat. These women even pay her. A miracle. She buys soap, toothpaste, and gets her shoes resoled. She sets part of her pay aside for her parents. When they finally manage to get out of Germany, Ilse wants to be able to support them.

* * * * *

Then she's sitting on a couch with Geoffrey Pittock-Buss, in his parents' living-room. They're holding hands. They kiss. Very cautiously. Geoffrey writes for the local paper. But he says he's different from most journalists. He doesn't smoke. He rarely goes to the pub. He attends church regularly and isn't in debt. One day, Geoffrey's going to ask Ilse to marry him.

In light of these developments, there's something she needs to teach herself. She needs to know more about certain things she currently knows nothing about. She has lived in three countries, she speaks three languages, but there are zones of her body, and words for these zones, and concepts for what could happen to these zones, and all of these are unknown to her. She's inhibited by her mother's admonishments. Agnes Gross always emphasized that there were certain bodily areas no-one should ever expose. Hygiene was the prime determinant of all human interaction and nobody in the Gross family ever strayed from the theory that children were produced by spiritual love between human beings. Officially, that is still the operating principle to which Ilse adheres.

She gets help from a bookcase she's supposed to dust. She finds a copy of Marie Stopes's book *Married Love* there. A paleobotanist, Stopes moved away from her research field to address applied sexuality. There is a bit of space between the bookcase and Ilse's employers' couch. The maid sits down on the floor. In a Northern climate, Stopes writes, women are apparently less prone to sexual arousal than in the South. A poem or a particularly pleasing memory, however, could lead even a British woman to want intercourse on a non-fertile day. 250 million spermatozoa can be found in an average ejaculation. The Queen of Aragon assumed that six incidences of sexual intercourse per day were necessary in a proper marriage. According to Stopes, this standard would kill the husbands of today.[14] Ilse is supposed to be dusting the bookshelf. She keeps reading.

* * * * *

In late August 1939, her employers give her money to go on a brief holiday. She's going to Hythe. She looks out of the train window. In a park, men are digging trenches. She's going past a jam factory. People pile sandbags in front of the factory gates.

In Hythe, she takes a room in a small bed and breakfast. She brings a book to the beach. She is reading Kenneth Graham's *The Wind in the Willows*. The mole does the spring cleaning, that's how the novel begins, and when he's done cleaning, he starts strolling around. It's a beautiful, sunny day, filled with joy. He moves aside the rabbit obstructing his path and enjoys how everyone's so busy – the birds with their nests, the flowers budding, the leaves growing – and only he, the mole, is lazy.[15]

Ilse takes a trip to Folkestone. She watches passengers leave the ferry from France. They seem a little downtrodden. She goes back to Hythe. She doesn't have lunch, because she wants to save money, for her parents once they finally arrive.

She's back from her brief holiday, in her London suburb, and it's either Thursday, August 31, or Friday, September 1, 1939, and from the window she sees the neighbor clipping his hedges when her parents call to say they will receive their visas for England very soon. It's all going to happen as planned. They're going to come over and then they'll wait together, as a family, for their U.S. visa.

Ilse cries tears of joy. She tells her parents to bring hedge clippers. They don't talk about what's going to happen to her sister. Her parents say: See you next week. She says: Hurry. She's looking out the window and the neighbor is still clipping. She reads Phyllis Bottome's novel *The Mortal Storm*. A young Jewish woman is engaged to a Nazi, then calls off the engagement, and tragedies ensue. The book makes Ilse cry.[16]

On Sunday morning, September 3, 1939, at 11:15 in the morning, Prime Minister Chamberlain announces on the radio that the war has begun. He explains what that means. There's a brief air raid alarm and then the Sunday roast and then Ilse goes for a walk in the sunny streets. She passes houses. She passes hedges. There will be no reunion with her parents.

3
***
Wind

In Douglas, on the Isle of Man, people now often congregate at the harbor. 1940 has begun. The islanders want to look at the foreigners. Ships from Liverpool come in. Germans, Austrians, and Italians get off. At first you only saw men. Now there are women as well. "Failt ort" means "Welcome" in the old language of the island. But hardly any Manx speak Manx anymore. At the Douglas harbor they shout: "Bloody Germans!" or "Nasty Germans!" Sometimes they whistle or spit in the direction of the arrivals.

The deportees carry their luggage from the dock to the train station. Most of them escaped Nazi persecution. Because many of them are Jewish, their fellow Germans in Germany categorized them as non-Germans. Now the insults at the harbor turn them back into Germans.

It is May 30, 1940, when Ilse Gross arrives in Douglas and boards the island train. The train starts to move. It's going twelve miles to the south. The internment camp for women is split between two towns. From Port St. Mary, you look out in the direction of England, and from Port Erin, towards Ireland. Ilse gets off at Port St. Mary. On the one hand, she's in a camp, surrounded by barbed wire. On the other hand, she's not in a camp. Like tourists, the interned will live in hotels and inns. That resembles the situation on the ship from Liverpool to Douglas. Even though it was transporting them to captivity, there was plenty of coffee on board, white cloths on the tables, and those bags the crew handed out to them. Lunch. They were treated well on the ferry. In every bag, a very decent sandwich, a hard-boiled egg, an apple, and an orange. And a cloth napkin.

* * * * *

Their hosts on the Isle of Man receive money from the British government, a fixed sum per person per day. For the innkeepers, that's not a bad deal. While tourists only visit in the summer, these guests may be staying for the entire duration of a World War. If you're smart and efficient, you can make this even more profitable. The deported will learn that some hosts are less generous than others.

Two inmates share one bed. That's the rule. Ilse has met a young woman on the ferry. They discovered that they had mutual acquaintances in Bingen. They sat next to each other on the train and admired the wildflowers of the Isle of Man. Now they'll share a mattress.

The interned are forbidden from owning candles. These could attract enemy airplanes. Maps aren't allowed either. The interned mustn't feed seagulls nor hang pictures on the walls of their rooms nor visit bars or dances nor buy alcoholic drinks. Bedtime at ten o'clock "and silence thereafter."[1]

✶ ✶ ✶ ✶ ✶

When the war started, the British government set up tribunals. These classified "enemy aliens" into three distinct categories.[2] Cases labelled "A" were unequivocal supporters of the Nazi regime. These foreign individuals were immediately deported. In Cardiff, for instance, a Jewish nurse attracted attention. She had only recently escaped from Germany and now wrote letters to her mother on a typewriter. Her fellow nurses had heard her typing. They found that suspicious. Clearly nurses don't type. So she received an "A."

The difference between category "B" (to be deported at a later date) and the seemingly unproblematic "C" (to be interned at some point) was incomprehensible in many cases. To some chairs of the tribunals, someone having family in Germany was enough to get them a "B" and not a "C." In most cases the refugee in question was frantic with worry about their family and wanted nothing more than to get them out of Germany, where they were living lives no human being should live. But that was all irrelevant.

When eighteen-year-old Ilse Gross from Bingen/Rhine appeared before a tribunal in Bromley/Kent, she didn't appear old enough for a "C." On October 30, 1939, she received a "B," because she was so young and easy to influence. But a "B" didn't seem all that bad at the time.

In the spring of 1940, German troops occupied Norway and Denmark. An attack on Great Britain seemed increasingly likely. Now every male refugee living close to the coast was interned. Categories didn't matter anymore.

At first, women and girls were seen as harmless. Then rumors circulated that some of these German maids spent suspicious amounts of time around military bases. And the other question arose – about secret codes and hanging up laundry. An important British diplomat said that "the paltriest kitchen maid with German connections" could be seen as dangerous for "the safety of the country." The government interned 8,000 men and 4,000 women. First, they took the women to prisons, then to the Isle of Man.[3]

＊ ＊ ＊ ＊ ＊

In the camp, hunger returns to Ilse's life. For lunch there's salted cod, sometimes herring, sometimes sardines. She hates fish, but of course she eats it. Once a week there's brawn. If you protest against brawn, they'll serve it twice a week. For supper there's two slices of white bread, a tomato, and a small piece of cheese. That's not enough for Ilse.

Port St. Mary has a beach. It's summer. Very few of the deported thought to bring bathing suits. They swim in their underwear. Do some of them run through the surf naked? That could be a rumor spread by the Manx.

The women gaze at the water and see a barbed wire fence. They would have to swim fifty miles through the Irish Sea to reach Liverpool, and the fence prevents any such attempt. At low tide it looks particularly striking.

English newspapers report that the German internees are enjoying a summer holiday financed by British taxpayers. There's a golf course on the campgrounds. The press writes stories about internees prancing around in the waves and holing balls on the greens and about upper-class enemy aliens having their golf clubs sent to their hotels. It's not long before they're denied access to the course.

＊ ＊ ＊ ＊ ＊

Among the internees is Jenny Fliess, cofounder of one of London's most revered vegetarian restaurants.[4] Friedelind Wagner is here, the grand-daughter of a German composer, and the actress Dora Lask, also known as Dora Diamant. She was Franz Kafka's last love. The artist Margarete Klopfleisch is pregnant when she arrives in the camp. She suffers a miscarriage and almost dies from the blood loss. On the island she will create a sculpture called "Desperation." It is a wooden figure, about a foot high: a screaming woman holding her arms above her head.[5]

There is reason to fear that the Germans are planning an invasion of the British Isles. They're in Paris. They might reach London. The government prints the brochure *If the Invader Comes: What to Do and How to Do It*. A rumor goes around that the Germans are planning to take Ireland first. From Ireland you can see the Isle of Man with your naked eye. If the German take Ireland, the Isle of Man will be their next stop, and thousands of Jewish men and women will fall into their hands. There's a suicide in the women's camp.[6]

The men are interned in the northern part of the island. Married couples are allowed to meet once a week, chaperoned. A man throws flowers over the fence to his fiancée and is sent to the island prison for three days.[7] From the men's camp, the government deports the deported once more: to Canada, to Australia. In the summer of 1940, hundreds of internees sail to Liverpool and are put onto the Arandora Star. The ship is scheduled to take them to Newfoundland. On July 2, as it's making its way northwest and has just reached the Outer Hebrides, a German torpedo hits it. More than 700 men drown. Once their identities have been verified, a vicar walks from inn to inn in Port St. Mary and Port Erin. He knocks on doors and shares the news with any of the wives, now widows, interned there.

* * * * *

In the camp, Jewish refugees and Germans who are Nazi sympathizers live very close to each other. In one of the inns, antisemites occupy the comfortably warm sitting room and make sure the Jewish internees remain in their unheated quarters. Eventually, the two parties are separated. In the hotel at the golf course, you only encounter Nazi women.[8] "My honey's a brownshirt" – that's a line you will hear there. And: "They're going to make it, just you wait and see."[9] People say that some women exclaim "Heil Hitler!" when they encounter Jewish internees in the street.[10]

You can walk around on the island, look at the fuchsia and the heather and try to ignore the barbed wire. Between Port Erin and Port St. Mary there's a spot where the sea hides from view, no matter where you look. All you see are trees, cows, farms, and you can imagine that you weren't deported to an island. There's a story of interned women walking around these paths, collecting gorse. And there's a lot of gorse on this island. These women carried the branches and walked home – whatever home means here – and arranged the branches just so, weaving them together, and when they were done with their enormous swastika of Isle of Man gorse, they put it on the dining room table at their inn and formed a circle around it and celebrated Germany and its dictator.[11]

* * * * *

Geoffrey sends letters from London. But he never comments on the war. If he did, these lines would be censored. Ilse used to send a letter to her parents every day. Now all she can do is write twenty-five words on Red Cross message forms every now and again. One of her cousins is interned in the men's camp, where his heart condition isn't treated. He dies on the Isle of Man.

* * * * *

The internees of the women's camp set up kindergartens and schools for the interned children. They run a university for the adults. Interned scholars lecture on history, theology, mathematics, Greek, German Literature, British History, and, in more general terms, "Problems of Life." There is one reading group that focuses exclusively on Goethe's *Faust*. Forty interned women are registered as volunteers for a research station in marine biology. A zoology student leads a group collecting seaweed.[12] The women inmates produce two different camp newspapers and both have a readership of exactly one person. The camp commandant, head censor, prohibits their publication.[13]

Ilse is a regular customer at the camp library, which exists because not all Britons despise the female inmates on the Isle of Man. Many books have been donated to the interned.[14] Ilse borrows novels. The lending rate is charged per day, so she does everything she can to finish each book within twenty-four hours. What she remembers most from these novels: detailed descriptions of opulent meals.

Back in Bingen, her father always read in his favorite armchair, his feet on a pouffe. In his hands he held his newspaper: *Frankfurter Zeitung*. On the armrest sat a camel-shaped ashtray. When he was done with the articles, he moved on to the crossword puzzle. Then he read a few articles in a science magazine. And smoked his cigar. In the music room, almost always empty, stood a Bechstein grand piano on a pale green, Chinese-style carpet.

Her mother liked sitting on the brown couch in front of the bookshelves. She read Thomas Mann's Joseph novels there, one after the other. She said Ilse could read anything she wanted, except for Tolstoy's *The Kreutzer Sonata*. That story was much too explicit, she said. And a respectable girl from Bingen on the Rhine only spent as much time in front of the mirror as it took to make sure her underskirt didn't show underneath her dress. If she looked at the mirror for any longer, she was a monkey.

It was always clear that Ilse wanted to be a writer. There was a brief phase in her childhood when she contemplated a medical career – but only for humanitarian reasons. Her literary oeuvre as a teenager consisted of various short stories, some poetry, and a few first chapters of novels written from the perspectives of animals.

When the three of them were sitting together, her father liked to read from his war diaries. 1914-1918. His medals: the Iron Cross Second Class. The Hessian Medal for Courage. The Honor Cross for Frontline Service. The dog who adopted him in Russia. He showed them the pictures. The dog. Ilse's father. Ilse's father on a horse. Strange trees. Advances and retreats. He told the story of how he had grown a beard and then shaved and how he put all the hair in an envelope and sent it to Ilse's mother. And the story of their honeymoon, long before the war, in 1905, in an open carriage travelling through the Po Valley, and the cheering Italians by the side of the road, waving German flags, how wonderful, astonishingly wonderful, even; albeit accidental, because the German Emperor and his wife were expected on their Italian tour and there was an uncanny resemblance – not between her mother and Empress Auguste Victoria, but between Ilse's fair-haired father and Kaiser Wilhelm II. And so Karl and Agnes Gross waved back to the cheering Italians.

* * * * *

Three interned women paid a fisherman five pounds each for him to take them over to Ireland. From Dublin they sent a postcard to camp commander Dame Joanna Cruikshank. That, too, may only be a rumor. But other stories start to circulate about escape plans. And so Dame Cruikshank feels the time has come to let everyone know what's wrong and what's right. As an entertaining warm-up segment to her speech in Port St. Mary's town hall, she schedules a "Baby Show." Mothers present their little children and this is supposed to fill the other internees with joy. Then the commandant talks about camp rules and the tightening of measures and the future loosening of these measures if internees should collectively exhibit the right kind of behavior. In conclusion, she says what she's been wanting to tell the women for a very long time. It doesn't matter where you are or what conditions you live in. Happiness, Dame Cruikshank tells the internees, is always something for which you yourself are responsible.[15]

* * * * *

Jewish internee Ilse Gross would like to convert. Christianity promises love and forgiveness on the Isle of Man. It seemed to foreground the law less than Judaism does. So it appears to her.

She could choose her fiancé's church: the Church of England. St. Mary's Church sits in the heart of Port St. Mary. But she wants to explore other options. She experiments with all the religious communities on her side of the barbed-wire fence: Baptists and Methodists and Seventh-day Adventists and Plymouth Brethren.

The Methodists win her over. The sermons are powerful. Laypeople speak. Everyone's welcome. The congregation sings with passion. She's looking for simple rituals, for a home. In Bingen, all the components of a Catholic procession signaled that a Jewish girl would never fully belong. Methodist services tell her the opposite. On Sundays she visits the chapel twice, once in the morning, once in the evening. She prays. She sings. She has less than perfect pitch. But it's enthusiasm that counts here. In September 1940, in the backroom of the chapel, she is baptized by the minister. For many years she's going to hold on to the certificate he hands her. Her faith won't last quite as long.[16]

* * * * *

Fiancé Geoffrey has sent her a really useful package: an 800-page literary history. Ford Madox Ford's *The March of Literature* begins in the times of King Amenhotep II, eighteen centuries before Christ, and concludes with Dostoevsky. Ford says there's no jingoism in claiming that seventeenth-century English poetry – say, George Herbert's – is the best writing ever produced in any country at any time.[17] Ilse loves George Herbert.

On the Isle of Man somebody advises her to stop writing poetry. As a non-native speaker, this person says, she'll never make it as a poet. Try prose. And *The March of Literature* states that the great narrative fiction of the future needs to fuse Dostoevsky's brilliant psychological insight and the impressionist techniques of the French – like Maupassant's. The author, Ford says, needs to be invisible: "to make you see."[18]

⋆ ⋆ ⋆ ⋆ ⋆

Ilse has three jobs now. She teaches German to the Methodist minister, she knits socks and sweaters, and she serves as the English teacher for a group of old German ladies. It's a rather complicated language. The "ough" in "though" is pronounced quite differently from the "ough" in "trough" or in "plough". As a textbook for her course, she uses *The March of Literature*.

She needs money for sanitary pads, toothpaste, shoe soles, and rolls from the bakery to stave off hunger. The menu at the inn hasn't changed much. She spends any spare pennies she has on concerts and lectures. Once a week, she walks to Port Erin and takes a sculpture course.

And then there are air raid alarms on the island. The Germans first attack London on Black Saturday, September 7, 1940. The Blitz begins. Almost every night throughout this autumn, German bombs fall on Great Britain. In the last four months of that year, 13,000 people die in London alone. When the wind is blowing from the East, internees think they can hear explosions in the cities on the coast. After attacking Liverpool, German planes fly back over the Irish Sea. Some people claim that German parachute troops have already landed in England.[19]

It's cold on the island. Internees discuss which inn makes life more bearable. Hot water is said to flow more frequently from the taps of the peach-colored Grand Hotel than from the ones in the smaller inns. Ilse's hosts are as stingy with coal as they are with food. Once they leave the house for church, one of the enemy aliens runs down to the coal cellar, comes back upstairs, and for a brief period it's a little warmer than usual.

In Bingen, autumn was the best season. Oxen pulled carriages laden with grapes through the gates of the house in Gaustraße. The oxen waited in the yard, the carriages were emptied, the oxen dropped pats, and someone fetched a hose to make the pats disappear. The three wine presses were running constantly. They were filled, emptied, filled again. In the cellars under the house, the juice would turn into wine. In the offices of Gross & Sons, secretaries sat in front of their typewriters and typed. The boys holding the oxen were the sons of the vintners from around Bingen and the wine merchants were the sons of the wine merchants before them.

Everyone knew everyone in Bingen. Phone numbers consisted of two digits. There was a tramline with one track. Ilse went to school with the daughters of the baker, the mailman, the photographer. How familiar it all was. And after 1933, in the shops and streets, everyone defined as "Aryan" knew exactly whom to ignore or insult.

As these autumn days ended, back in a different age, the potato peeling machine was running in the kitchen and the goulash was cooking on the stove and then the potatoes as well, and in the yard, at long tables, sat the vintners and the helpers and the wine merchants, her father and her two uncles, the most authentic Bingeners anyone could imagine. Then food was put on the table. And at sunrise the next grape-laden ox cart turned into Gaustraße and rolled into the yard.

These are Ilse's memories of the wonderfully harmonious world of non-Jewish vintners and Jewish wine merchants. The stories are true. And they're also inaccurate. Long before 1933, companies like Gross & Sons, in Bingen and elsewhere, had been the targets of antisemitic smear campaigns. Newspapers took swipes at small-town Jewish merchants. They spun conspiracy theories of Jews following systematic plans intent on destroying German wine regions. Numerous court trials took place: Jewish businesses were suspected of turning "natural wine" into "artificial wine." One paper used a well-known psalm and altered it slightly: "At the Rivers of Babylon they sat and wept, at the Wine Rivers of Germany they sit and dilute." That's how German Jews were attacked around 1900.[20]

* * * * *

It's winter on the Isle of Man. Chimneys break off in the storm. Ilse is walking to the post office to pick up Geoffrey's Christmas package. On the way she's blown to the ground. She's lying on the street, on her back. She gets up. She struggles onwards. To her, this seems symbolic. There's George Herbert's "The Affliction (I)," a poem about a person descending from a happy life with "furniture so fine," with "flow'rs and happiness," and "glorious household-stuff." In 1633 Herbert imagined how this individual remembers the happy times and becomes acquainted with pain and grief, and then turns "thin and lean" in the "storm and wind." And still that person won't let go of their belief in God. Or will they? The last line runs: "Let me not love thee, if I love thee not."[21] You could ponder that one for quite a long time.

✳ ✳ ✳ ✳ ✳

By the spring of 1940, in Bingen, the Bechstein grand piano no longer stands in the music parlor. Karl and Agnes Gross now share the flat with other Jewish families and have moved to the small room in which Ilse's governess once slept. Eventually Ilse's parents will move to Frankfurt and find a room there.

Now the piano, other furniture, and carpets are sitting in a container in Rotterdam. The container was filled because the family believed they would finally escape to the United States. It's still waiting when the Germans bomb Rotterdam on May 14, 1940. Along with much of the city, they destroy the Gross family's container and the Bechstein inside.

✳ ✳ ✳ ✳ ✳

Late in 1940, tribunals take place on the Isle of Man. Committees decide who'll get to leave the camps as a free person. Since the sinking of the Arandora Star, fewer British politicians believe in interning refugees.[22]

Before they're released, 4,000 women must be interviewed. Every day new lists of names appear in the shop window of the Port St. Mary grocery store. If you find your name on it, you must be ready by the next morning, get on the police-escorted bus to Douglas, answer questions, come back to the women's camp and then wait a few weeks for the tribunal's decision. Some interviewers are charming, others gruff. Nothing is ever certain. Some Jewish women are forced to stay on the island, some Nazi women sail off to Liverpool and freedom.[23]

On a Friday morning, December 17, 1940, Ilse Gross takes the bus to Douglas. She appears before the tribunal. She's taken back to the camp. Two months and one week later, Dora Diamant, known as "Dora Kafka" on the Isle of Man, presents a musical afternoon at a school in Port Erin. The program consists of Jewish folk songs and anecdotes, motives from *The Dybbuk* and Hasidic melodies. The event begins at 3:30 in the afternoon. If she felt like it, Ilse Gross could go. She's still interned.[24]

4

London

She puts on a pink dress and dons a navy-blue hat. The seams of her dress are also navy blue. Ilse Gross, who has just turned twenty, has been freed from internment "until further order of the court." On February 4, 1941, they allowed her to go from the ninth biggest to the biggest British Isle. Now it's a Saturday in March, and, since her father can't be here, a minister of Elmers End Free Church walks beside her as she enters West Wickham's Anglican church. She's holding the *Book of Common Prayer*. Geoffrey's brother is best man.

Soon the readers of West Wickham's local newspaper will learn about the wedding, the dress, the seams, the hat, the best man, and the prayer book. The piece runs under the heading "Refugee Bride." The daughter of "Mr. and Mrs. Karl Gross," the paper states, is "a refugee from Nazi oppression." After a reception at the groom's parents' house, the couple leaves West Wickham for Northwood, Middlesex. That's according to the knowledge of the *Bromley & District Times*.

It is safe to assume that Ilse now shares a bed with Geoffrey. For nine months her fellow internee used to lay next to her, on the same mattress. Now things are different.

She has handed in her "Aliens Registration Book." She has a British Identity Card. Another new life is beginning. Because they fear a German invasion, many Jewish refugees take on new names in Britain. Some also want to make their names easier to pronounce. Abrahamson turns into Ambrose, Rosenthal into Rosen.[1] In her case, that's not necessary. At least for the time being, she's Mrs. Geoffrey Pittock-Buss.

The newlyweds return from Northwood. They move in with Geoffrey's parents. Then they find their own flat. There's an expression, "non-blitzers," for those seemingly non-heroic individuals who moved to London after the worst bombings were over.[2] There's no specific term for newcomers who missed out on the horrors because they were living behind barbed wire.

And the attacks continue. Ilse survives the night which becomes known as "The Wednesday," from March 19 to March 20, 1941, when German planes destroy much of the East End. It brings the heaviest bombardment in terms of tons. She also survives the "Full Moon," in mid-May 1941, when the House of Commons burns and 1,400 Londoners lose their lives.[3]

∗ ∗ ∗ ∗ ∗

She's not a maid anymore. She's her husband's secretary. Geoffrey still writes for newspapers. He has also founded an organization supporting international understanding and a small press publishing anti-war literature. And he's a member of the pacifist Peace Pledge Union and an activist in the Indian Freedom Campaign. He climbs onto a box in Hyde Park and calls for the end of British colonial rule.

After a while, Ilse learns that her restless husband would like them to have an open marriage. He has already found a candidate to pursue this project with, a woman working in a newspaper office. Her husband and the candidate are going off for a weekend together. Ilse isn't convinced. Nonetheless she sleeps with a friend, if only to prove that she's not old-fashioned.

And then she leaves Geoffrey and looks for a room of her own. She finds one. The landlady tells her she's going to keep a share of Ilse's income. A misunderstanding: Ilse doesn't want to live in a brothel. She keeps looking. She's successful in Bayswater, close to Kensington Gardens. The building is quiet and clean. From her window she has a nice view of a church spire. That's going to change.

She arranges her own books on her own bookshelf, mounts her own art prints on the wall and fries eggs on her own hot plate. For the first time she gets to live by herself. There's always hot running water here. What an incredible luxury. While she sleeps, she holds her purse containing her ID card, her money, and her ration book. She always has her best dresses ready, so that she can save them in case of an attack. The bombs keep falling. Soon the church spire disappears.

The landlady says she doesn't mind gentlemen visitors. But this is still a respectable house, she points out. It's exciting, magical even – as Ilse Pittock-Buss will later write, under a different name – to emerge from the underground, perhaps with a lover, and watch the searchlights in the sky, to see a darkened car creep by. She's English. She's not an "enemy alien." Her bed is a bit small for two. But that doesn't matter much.

A couple, two women, live in the flat on the ground floor. During air raids it's safer downstairs, so everyone climbs from their beds and comes down the stairs. One young woman is always the last to show up, and there's this soldier who's always with her. His uniform is tan, his hair blonde. After a while, Ilse realizes that it's not always the same soldier. The shoulder stripes aren't the same. She's seen different fair-haired soldiers. This helps Ilse lose her inhibitions. Before long, she also brings company.

On couches, in armchairs and on the floor, they wait, in silence. On these nights, you don't hear a thing from houses in London. No music, no voices. And everything is dark. No rays of light. The city's will to survive finds expression in the will to stay home.[4]

✳ ✳ ✳ ✳ ✳

In the spring of 1933, the Jewish girls of Bingen formed a Zionist club. The supposedly Aryan students were taking "race science" classes in the early afternoon. The non-Aryans were sent home early. It felt good to put on a blue skirt and a white blouse and to make plans for a Jewish state. It felt good to admire Theodor Herzl. The Hitler Youth marched through Gaustraße. They sang: "Heads are rolling, Jews are weeping" because they knew that most of the Jewish families of Bingen lived in this neighborhood. Physical work was utterly foreign to Ilse. For a while, though, she dreamed of joining a kibbutz, as a tiller of the fields, in a country free from antisemites.

✳ ✳ ✳ ✳ ✳

First, she was a Zionist, then a Methodist. Now she's a pacifist. That's a complicated stance to take in wartime England. A writer named John Middleton Murry leads the peace movement. He thinks it's unnecessary for the Americans to join the war. Whatever's happening to the Jews in German-occupied Europe, Murry claims, can't be all that terrible.[5]

Ilse's still friends with Geoffrey. She works for him, she studies Gandhi, as he does, and she's convinced that passive resistance and civil disobedience are more effective tools than military warfare. She reads Aldous Huxley, who believes modern man to be empty and his life meaningless. Huxley says that all people do now is play games or consume sports and other silly entertainment. And because these external stimuli don't fill the emptiness, Huxley states, people fall for war propaganda. Love and mindfulness: these are the virtues Huxley finds important.[6] That makes sense to Ilse.

She spends a lot of time in pubs with the pacifists. As beer is rationed, at some point in the evening they must move on to less trustworthy drinks, like sloe gin, for example, until, eventually, there's no sloe gin either. Even then they stay in the pub because it's far too boring at home.

On a summer evening in 1943, some of her friends give a party. The radio's broadcasting Arsenal vs. Charlton. The final score: 7:1. Huxley would probably classify all these eight goals as "external stimuli" that people use to try to fill their empty lives. Late that night, another friend joins them. He's still excited. He was there, at the Southern Final of the English Football League War Cup. At Wembley. "At" Wembley? Until that moment, Ilse had thought that "wembley" was a verb. "To wembley." Apparently it's a football stadium. People cried at Wembley, this friend says, soldiers in uniform and pacifists like him, all in tears in the stands when they sang "Abide with Me." 70,000 people, imagine that. "When other helpers fail and comforts flee / Help of the helpless, oh, abide with me." In Germany the masses are singing different songs.

* * * * *

Her father used to sit in the cafe in Bingen every day, with his brother Isidor, and Marx, his brother-in-law. For Karl Marx, that was a last name – for her uncle, his first. The three men always played the card game *Skat*, never a different game. She remembers how one of the men often threw his cards down on the table, though the game had only just begun, because he knew by looking at them how it was all going to turn out.

* * * * *

Since March 1943 Ilse has been working as the secretary of the Indian Freedom Campaign Committee. In an office near Euston Station, she sits in meeting after meeting and minutes the debates about how India's freedom could be attained.

She doesn't know anything about her unfree parents' situation. In December 1942 the foreign secretary Anthony Eden officially condemned the mass killings of European Jews. Since then, the news has become more and more gruesome. She can only expect the worst.[7]

Walking home from work, Ilse Pittock-Buss passes Marylebone Library, steps inside, and makes a major discovery: Henry James's *The Sacred Fount*, first published in 1901. Elegant prose. Long, complicated sentences. Sophisticated protagonists involved in rambling conversations. The library's windows are blacked out. Ilse sits at one of the tables, James's novel in her hand. She feels very grown-up. Finally, she's able to get an education.

There's this first-person narrator you don't learn anything about, not even his name. And he's going to the country for the weekend, to some social event. On the train he encounters the problem he's going to have to deal with for the next three hundred pages. Why does Mrs. Brissenden suddenly look so much younger? Why does Mr. Brissenden seem so much older? And what connects these phenomena? Nothing more dramatic will happen in *The Sacred Fount*. For days protagonists discuss the Brissenden question. "Quoi donc?" somebody asks, in the most refined fashion, when the narrator seems to have reached a new stage in his research, but all he answers is: "I'll tell you tomorrow. Good night" and a chapter ends and a new one begins and that, too, won't bring significant results. A critic said that in this novel James was trying to make "nothing out of nothing."[8]

In the next seven years Ilse will be busy working her way through Henry James's oeuvre: twenty novels and more than one hundred tales. His fiction foregrounds fine sensitivity. Gripping plot development? Not so much. What's important is how you perceive the world and every emotional movement, whether found in yourself or observed in others. Behind the art of literature, James says, we need a writer "on whom nothing is lost."[9]

* * * * *

In June 1944, walking down Tottenham Court Road, Ilse's attention is drawn by a strange noise. She hears people sweeping away the shards of broken windowpanes, that is familiar, but there's also this monstrous dark sound in the sky. She has survived the "Baby Blitz." January to April 1944, fourteen nights of bombing. Now the Germans send their unmanned rockets: the V-1, the V-2. People say that if you hear a V-2 it means you either survived it or you're already dead. On Tottenham Court Road, Ilse stays alive.

On March 8, 1945, a rocket hits Smithfield, the London meat market. People were waiting in long queues there. 110 of them are killed. Later in March a hospital is destroyed, a church, houses in Stepney. 140 people lose their lives. On April 1, 1945, a V-2 crashes down into a garden in Orpington, close to West Wickham, where Geoffrey's parents live, and Ivy Millichamp, thirty-four years old, is standing in the kitchen of her bungalow (her husband Eric is sleeping, he's been working night shifts) and the explosion kills Mrs. Millichamp. She's the last British civilian to lose her life in World War Two.[10]

On May 8, 1945, Winston Churchill speaks on the radio. He says: "This is your hour." He says it's not the "victory of a party or of any class," but the triumph of the "great British nation as a whole." He appears on the balcony of the Ministry of Health. The masses down on the square are singing "For He's a Jolly Good Fellow."

And then red velvet adorns the balcony of Buckingham Palace. The Royal Family show themselves that evening. For today the government has lifted the rationing of beer, so many Londoners are quite drunk. Inflated condoms are floating through the streets like balloons. The king has put on a navy uniform with golden tresses. Princess Elizabeth, who has just turned nineteen, is wearing the uniform of the Auxiliary Territorial Service. Every time the Windsors make a move to leave the balcony, the crowd shouts "We want the King," and the Royals stay out for a little while longer.[11]

* * * * *

You hear the word "Belsen" all the time. British forces liberated the camp. Now there are the most horrible, unimaginable reports in newspapers and magazines and in cinema newsreels. Years later, English school children will shout "Belsen" if one of their fellow pupils seems overly thin. Many people will remember the pictures of the emaciated corpses and survivors for the rest of their lives.

At this time, in Great Britain, the term "Belsen" represents all the crimes committed by Nazi Germany. The names of other camps rarely appear in the press. Postwar British media don't highlight the fact that most Belsen victims were Jewish. Nor do they explore that Belsen functioned as just one element of an immense genocidal system. Nothing's supposed to distract from Great Britain's military triumph.[12]

In the summer of 1945 Ilse goes off on holiday. She hitch-hikes to the Wye. The river originates in Plynlimon, flows through the Welsh moors, veers northeast at Aberllynfi and then flows into England, passing the ruins of Tintern Abbey. Wordsworth wrote poems there and Turner worked on paintings.

Ilse reads Henry Green's *Loving* on the Wye. The novel has just come out. It's set in the summer of 1941. Green tells the stories of servants in an Irish country house that belongs to an English family. She's twenty-four years old when she reads the novel. When she's eighty-five, she will find an article about Green in the *Times Literary Supplement* and cut it out and mail it to a friend. Nobody knows Green anymore, she will write in the accompanying note. She read Green back then, she says, and sixty years later she still remembers exactly how it felt.

Green makes the butler, the cook, the maids come alive. *Loving* isn't social reportage about the life of the lower classes. It's psychological fiction. Green seems to understand the servants completely: their strengths, their weaknesses, their desires, their fears. Two maids pull the sheets off a bed in their mistress's bedroom, because the mistress has lost her sapphire ring and the servants must look for it. One of the maids is standing on one side of the bed and the other is standing on the other and one of them tells the other that she is secretly in love with the butler – "I love Charley Raunce, I love 'im I love 'im" – and that she would cut open the veins of her right arm for that man. Then she leaves the room. The other maid stays behind and says, to herself really, that she had known this all along. That it wasn't such a big secret. Her face shows pain. And she's standing in an empty bedroom that's not hers.[13]

* * * * *

At Bloomsbury House you can find information on who survived the German camps. It's the headquarters of Jewish aid organizations in London. Ilse goes. She waits in line. She steps into the building. It's crowded with people. She walks from room to room, looking at the walls and lists of names. She has saved money, whenever possible, to support her parents. But what would she do if they really had survived? If they came to London, as old, broken victims? It's clear to her how different the real survivors would be from the comforting parents of her dreams. She doesn't find their names.

A little later, in October 1945, she starts working as a secretary for the psychoanalyst Kate Friedlander, formerly Käte Frankl of Innsbruck, then Berlin, now London. Friedlander studies delinquent youth. It is important, she points out, to understand the needs of young people today. Their emotional development suffered because family life in war times was so unstable, so to Friedlander, these young people are just as much war victims as any wounded soldier. Now it's crucial to help them become "useful citizens."[14] Friedlander's new secretary, twenty-four years old, types up these findings.

* * * * *

Ilse titles one of her first short stories "Adolescence." As a writer, she calls herself Kathrine Pittock. Her English is simple and clear. Writing in German is not an option. Her story portrays a young woman, a maid, who's going to the park with the child in her charge. In the park, in "the hungry hour before lunch," the maid's thinking about poetry. She meets a young man. She looks into his blue eyes, and her life could change now, at this moment, but then she thinks his eyes are a bit too blue and springtime too emotional. This young woman doesn't have emotions. "I live at the bottom of the sea," she says. At night the past comes back to her: a meadow in the heat of the summer, a linden tree in bloom, a warm, brown room. Where the young woman lived back then the story doesn't reveal. Her present seems very British. It is a world of buses, teapots, and parks.[15]

* * * * *

She moves to Horsham, twenty-five miles from London. Now Ilse works as a secretary in a mental health clinic for adolescents. Kate Friedlander has taken her along.

After work Ilse queues up in front of grocers. She holds her ration book in her hand. Even for onions, she has to wait. The Horsham cinema shows war movies: monumental heroic stories. They're not Ilse's thing. From time to time, if she's lucky, they show Italian neorealism.

One day Ilse goes to London and places her hand on a telephone book. Geoffrey and she are getting a divorce, in November 1946. As there's no bible, they improvise.

In Horsham she needs to be quick if she wants new books. Paper is rationed. Whenever there's a new issue of *Penguin New Writing*, she walks from the clinic to the bookshop in her lunch break, buys a copy, walks back, flicks through it as she's walking, then, after work, reads all the short stories, poems, essays in one sitting and then reads them all again. In *Penguin New Writing* a critic named Walter Allen says that Henry Green should be seen as the only real artist in British literature. All the other writers, Allen proclaims: too politicized, too autobiographical. Green you don't find in his works. You find him outside of them.[16]

* * * * *

In February 1947 the sun stops shining. Maybe forever. The longest sunless period ever recorded in England begins. It's freezing cold. The British Isles are hit by one snowstorm after the other. And there's not enough coal. A natural disaster meets an energy crisis. Gas is rationed. The government shuts down the electricity for five hours each day. They make an exception for hairdressers, whose electric perm machines may be used without interruption. But neon signs have to be turned off. And newspapers are smaller now. People are cold in their flats and houses. They drink more because it makes them feel warmer, but then alcohol production is curbed. Dog racing is prohibited. The Big Ben clock stops in the cold. Three million people lose their jobs, and the British Minister for Energy is one of them. It was him, people say, who failed to order enough coal.[17]

* * * * *

When spring arrives, Ilse turns twenty-six. She keeps typing case studies of problematic youth. The snow is melting. Some of the worst floods in British history wreak havoc. At night, Ilse sits at home, trying to write a novel. But she can't. She needs more time. And Victor Lehmann, a London lawyer, forwards some letters from Deutsche Bank in Bingen to her. She doesn't understand the letters and mails them back to him.

On an April morning in 1947 she is sitting at breakfast. There is toast and marmalade on the table, this she will remember for her entire life, and there's another envelope from Lehmann. She picks it up. She opens it.

Lehmann writes that her parents have died: her father on February 1, 1944, her mother on October 9, 1944. He doesn't have more information. And she must have already heard about this. Lehmann's letter states that the "sad news" that she "had already received through friends has been officially confirmed." She is surprised by how cool she is and how she actually feels relief. She wonders how inhuman that is – to have that emotion inside of her. She tries to mourn her parents, but she can't. She has already mourned them when they were still alive.

She wants to make a new start and Horsham isn't the right place. She still has the jewelry her mother once gave her for emergencies. She writes to Lehmann that she's thinking about selling these pieces. And that she doesn't know how. She asks whether it's very thoughtless of her to bother him with this question, but, she says: "I have no-one else to advise me."

* * * * *

On April 21, 1947, Princess Elizabeth is calling from South Africa. She's sitting at a garden table, in a short-sleeved white dress. She's wearing a deceptively simple necklace around her neck and in front of her there's a BBC microphone and her manuscript and a small silver paperweight on the pages.

The princess speaks on the occasion of her twenty-first birthday. First, she stresses how wonderful her travels to Rhodesia and South Africa have been and how much these places felt like "home." Visiting Africa, the royal family travelled in a luxury train consisting of fourteen carriages. In the languages of the ruling minorities in South Africa, it was called "The White Train" or "Die Wittrein."

Then the princess addresses the young people of her generation. Now, she says, is the time to become adults. The war years are over, and the moment has arrived to take the weight off their parents' shoulders. The princess promises her listeners to always serve them and the great imperial family. She's ready to serve for her entire life, however short or long it might be.[18]

* * * * *

Ilse quits her job. She keeps her mother's emerald ring. She sells all the other pieces. She wants to go away, as far as possible. She wants to take the typewriter along and do nothing but write. A novel. She's done the math: If she doesn't spend more than three pounds per week, she'll be able to make it through a few months. She goes to London and gets advice from her friends. Maybe Shaftesbury? There's something about Shaftesbury she finds attractive. It's an old town on a hill. But the pacifists advise against it. They say the men there would ogle her all the time. In Shaftesbury she wouldn't be able to go to a pub without them making advances. Going to Cornwall seems like the right choice. The pacifists say there are no importunate men in Cornwall. That prognosis will turn out to be incorrect.

5

Cornwall

In Mevagissey, a fishing village, Ilse walks into the only café in town, asks for a room, finds a room, and places her typewriter on the table. Then she gets to know the bohemians of the village. These are people who aren't just writers; they're published writers. She's so amazed. There's this man who lives here, Louis Adeane, and he has a book out that people can actually buy and which has his name on the cover. *The Night Loves Us: Thirty-Two Poems*. There's another man named Sydney whose pen name is W.S. Graham and you can see that name on the covers of three books. Three. Sydney's married to Nessie. In another life, Sydney was an engineer and Nessie a comptometer operator. Now they're both poets. Unlike Sydney, Nessie is still unpublished. Ilse begins to detect a certain pattern in the lives of the creative men and women of her time.

They're all poor in Mevagissey. Ilse shares what she has with Nessie and Sydney. Sometimes the fishermen give them prawns. Ilse takes it as a given that the fishermen whistle when she walks by. So as not to distract the churchgoers, there's an unwritten law that women mustn't swim in the harbor on Sundays. Once a week, Nessie, Sydney, and Ilse buy a piece of meat that they roast in the community oven. When it's done, Ilse takes the roast out, the meat steaming in the roasting tin, next to the potatoes, and she walks down the village street carrying the hot food, its scents rising before her.

＊ ＊ ＊ ＊ ＊

Her English may still give away that she's from the Continent. But she probably doesn't talk much about her family history. And it's likely that now, in the summer of 1947, the people she meets here don't know much about the destruction of the European Jews. After the reports of 1945 public interest in the atrocities has faded away. In the boiled-down version of the British press, the Germans are sadists and always will be. That's all one needs to know. In the autumn of 1945, articles about the Nuremberg Trials appeared in the papers and then quickly disappeared again. Paper is still rationed. There's simply no space for stories about such tedious affairs.

The word "Holocaust" will only come into use decades later. Some journalists and scholars are already exploring the systematic genocide, but their work doesn't reach a wider audience. Most conversations about the war revolve around the heroic endurance of the British people. In one part of London, activists walk around collecting signatures. There's not enough housing in Hampstead. They want Jewish refugees to go back to where they came from.[1]

＊ ＊ ＊ ＊ ＊

Often Ilse and the other bohemians of Mevagissey lean against the wall down at the harbor and watch what the fishermen are up to. How they repair their boats. How they mend nets. How they play water polo in leopard-patterned swimming trunks.

Ilse's typewriter now sits on top of the wardrobe in her room. She doesn't use it much. Sometimes she types up Sydney's poems. Sometimes poets or painters come and she cuts their hair. Once the fishermen let her come out with them. Usually, they don't want women on their boats, but they make an exception for her.

And then George Barker comes to Mevagissey. He's a man from a different universe. She meets him, and that has serious repercussions.

George Barker, thirty-four years old, is the greatest poet of his generation. The monumental T.S. Eliot has called him a genius. He has also won the praise of W.B. Yeats. His poems are mythical, sensuous, surreal, sometimes complicated, sometimes banal. He writes lines about the desert in his heart and the hyaenas howling in that desert. George Barker taught literature in Tokyo and has lived in New York and now he's giving Mevagissey a chance. Ilse, the future Ilse Barker, says: When he's standing in the pub with his cap on his head he looks like an Irish laborer – and when he's lying on the beach he looks like a Greek god.

The bohemians and the fishermen play darts in the pub and buy one another rounds of beer. Ilse notices that the fishermen's wives never show up. In the public life of the village, you only see them on Sundays, with their husbands and children, on the way to church and back.

And the way the writers and artists of Cornwall define gender roles is only slightly less conventional. Ilse meets David the painter and his girlfriend Lali. David has studied art in London, at the Slade. That's very impressive. Lali studied there too. Just as impressive. But people only talk about David's art and never about Lali's. David gets a little bit of money from his mother. Because it's not enough to survive on, Lali takes the bus every day and waits tables somewhere and then takes the bus back. David gets to stay at home and paint. That's how things work.

* * * * *

The Irish worker and Greek god is one of very few well-known English poets of his time who doesn't have an upper-class background. George Barker's father was unemployed for what seemed like forever and his mother, people say, took her wedding band to the pawnshop every Wednesday. When he was fifteen, George realized that he had to become a very important poet, so he put on a long coat and a very big hat. He's since changed his attire, but now, in 1947, he's very important indeed. He's anarchic, never moderate, never calm. He cleans out the dregs of cigarette lighters and inhales them. He drinks. A lot. He's witty and angry and very interesting. He's Catholic, and, as kitchen-sink psychology has it, that means he's on a constant guilt trip, but he feels even more guilty because he took out his little brother's eye in a fencing accident when he was a boy. George despises his father, who ended up finding a job after all, as a butler, and worships his Irish mother, nicknamed "Big Mumma," who never gets up in the cinema when they play "God Save the King."[2]

In comparison to his mother, says one of his poems, every other person seems "like a little dog following a brass band." Is that why no woman will ever tame his restlessness? Perhaps. Over the course of his life George Barker is going to father fifteen children with four different women, and now, in the summer of 1947, seven of these children – some by his wife, some by his long-time girlfriend – are already in or on their way into this world. And a new, additional girlfriend also enriches George Barker's life.[3]

He has come to Mevagissey without his wife, his girlfriends, his children or his mother. He probably seems free here, as free as Ilse Pittock-Buss. She watches him in the pub. He's singing and accompanying himself on an imaginary violin. He sings "Careless Love." Much later, someone will say that Ilse and George embodied two different principles. She was rational and controlled. He was the exact opposite.

* * * * *

Four years later Ilse will sell the manuscript of her first novel to a major New York publishing house. The novel will be set in Cornwall, in a small village by the sea. It will tell the story of a young woman who felt constrained in London. Her name is Veronica. Her black hair used to be long, and her clothes once seemed girlish. These times are over. In the very first chapter, Veronica, though on a quest for solitude, looks out at the harbor with a man at her side. Her haircut may seem unconventional, but she lets this man explain the beauties and mysteries of Cornwall to her, all in elaborate detail. He talks about the herons flying up from the marshes and the stone circles left by the ancient druids and the blooming of the heather. He says that August is the only unbearable time here. Too many tourists. She enjoys his poetic descriptions of Cornwall's flowers: the sea pink, the bluebells. She wanders along the coast with this man until he takes her hand in his and says "Veronica, I love you" and calls her "my beautiful." They find a place on the cliffs where nobody can see them. She feels the rough grass and the uneven ground beneath her and afterwards tears flow and he kisses her and asks whether he scared her, and then, in the following days, she feels stronger than ever before.

* * * * *

With one of his pals, George visits Ilse's friends Sydney and Nessie. At the dinner table Nessie tells a story, an entertaining one, and this story takes a while. George thinks Nessie's being vivacious only because he's there. He turns to his friend and he whispers: "She's a whore."[4] Either George Barker thinks that each and every woman of this era only wants to have sex with him, or he believes that the women of British bohemia shouldn't talk too much. Probably both of these options apply.

Then the Greek god leaves Mevagissey. He has told Ilse about his brother, the victim of the fencing accident, the one with the glass eye. A painter. A one-eyed painter? Ilse finds this interesting. George asks whether it would be okay if his brother got in touch. He says his brother lives in Newlyn, not too far away. And when George's brother sends a postcard, his name is Albert, but everyone calls him Kit, and he asks whether he might stop by, Ilse writes back that there's an empty room on the top floor of her inn.

When the bus arrives, she walks down the street to the bus stop. The first passengers begin to disembark and walk towards her. She wonders which one of them might be Kit, and then she spots this young man who looks like George and doesn't look like George, who has brighter hair than George, more hair than George, blue eyes that are not quite as bright as George's. He wears horn-rimmed glasses and a brown corduroy jacket.

In the evening they go to the pub together. The next morning, she doesn't see him at the inn. She strolls through the village, looking for him. He's leaning against the harbor wall, looking out to sea. She decides to wait for him to speak to her. She also leans against the wall. He doesn't give the slightest sign of having noticed her. Then he turns and walks away.

* * * * *

In Liverpool's shop windows, there are now signs that read: "We are not Jews." Shop owners have put them up to save their businesses from looting and destruction.

Across England, it is the summer of antisemitic riots. In Palestine, Jewish partisans and British soldiers are fighting each other. The state of Israel doesn't yet exist. After every guerrilla mission the English press calls for Jewish Brits to denounce the partisans' actions. It seems like every Jew in the United Kingdom is held personally responsible for what's happening in the Middle East. Then British troops execute a Jewish underground fighter and Jewish fighters kill two British officers. The press reports on the incident and displays pictures. The *Daily Express* says the actions of the Jewish terrorists are incomparable to the atrocities committed by the Nazis; incomparable, the paper states, because they're worse. And then, on an August weekend in 1947, youths maraud through Jewish neighborhoods in Manchester, London, Glasgow, Liverpool. They destroy shops and cemeteries. They attack synagogues.[5] It's questionable whether Ilse knows anything about this. She and her friends probably can't afford newspapers.

Kit ignored her at the harbor. But when she runs into him later, he seems happy to see her. They go for a cup of coffee and suddenly there's nothing remote about him at all. Now she finally remembers what his brother told her. She must have been standing to the side of his glass eye. They go to the beach together and he falls asleep, and she notices that between his eyelids on one side, there's a tiny gap.

Kit stays for a few days. Then he leaves. Then he comes back. He makes drawings of fighting Amazons. Ilse has worked for a psychoanalyst for years, so these pictures of imposing women give her food for thought. At night, she puts a saucer next to her bed. That's where Kit puts his glass eye.

Then he goes back to Newlyn and writes to her, every day. He tells her that the people he's sharing an old loft with are going to move out soon, and he wonders whether she might want to move in with him. The moment these people have gone, he sends her a telegram asking whether she'd like to live with him for a week. After that week, he says, they could see how things are going.

She takes the bus and then the train to Newlyn, further West, to the most remote corner of Cornwall. In Kit's enormous room, old, bleached sails hang from the ceiling. The sails are the walls of his flat, he says. You can see the harbor from the loft and the wide bay. She looks around and she doesn't see an easel. There is none. This painter can't afford an easel. He also can't afford paints. Ilse goes back to Mevagissey.

She picks up her things. Then she buys a double bed from a scrap dealer, and has it delivered to the loft in Newlyn. The bedsprings can be noisy, in certain situations. Even if Kit Barker isn't painting now and hasn't been painting for a while, Ilse doesn't question for one second that he's a painter. She hasn't published anything. And yet, she's a writer.

Kit is so shy – except when he's alone with her. Sometimes he's so timid that he can't even enter a shop. As a child he wrote an adventure novel. He had a communist phase, sold the *Daily Worker*, and then began to produce surrealist paintings. He never went to art school. He feels inferior to artists who did. He was an engineer in the army. They discharged him shortly before the war was over. Psychological reasons. What reasons exactly? He doesn't want to talk about that time.

Ilse keeps reading Henry James – and now Joseph Conrad, too. Józef Teodor Nałęcz Konrad Korzeniowski started learning English at the age of twenty-one, and he's one of the great stylists of English literature. Maybe she's drawing parallels.

Kit reads history books. To Ilse that's a complete waste of time. She doesn't want to know about battles or wars, winners or losers. She says it doesn't do anyone any good. On the wireless they listen to Shakespeare plays, hoping the batteries will last until the fifth act is over. In the evenings they go to the pub. Saturday nights they go dancing.

Then they're forced to leave the loft because it's going to be turned into a sardine cannery. They move northwards to a little house on the moor, above Zennor, half an hour on foot from the nearest bus stop. You can see a tiny sliver of the Atlantic from there. The privy isn't close to the house, and it's a difficult route when it's foggy.

There's no path up to where they live, so they always walk through the soggy fields. They have bought second-hand wellingtons, with lots of holes. They use bicycle repair patches to cover them, and these patches fall off very quickly, so their feet are always wet. They carry coal up to the house and rechargeable radio batteries in the other direction. There's no electricity and no running water. All they have is a rain barrel.

Another painter lives close by. Sometimes he invites Kit and Ilse to use his bathtub. When they're walking at night, they always carry a lamp. There are old mining shafts everywhere that you really don't want to fall into. They keep a small candle burning in the window of their home when they're out. This tiny light is what they make their way towards when they return home, freshly bathed.

Together they sit at their round table. Ilse writes. Kit paints if there's money for paint. He paints fishermen and their nets and their boats. He paints skulls washed ashore: horse skulls, cow skulls. He paints on fertilizer bags that he mounts on frames. Sometimes he just paints on boards he finds somewhere, but he says he likes the sensuous flexibility of the sacks. Decades later Ilse will write extensively about these details of Kit's artistic production. About her own craft, as an author, she won't reveal much.

* * * * *

There are bluebells on their hill. But Ilse's writing a short story about a young woman who gets killed in the London tube. There's a haggard young man yelling that he pushed her in front of the train. The police take him away.

She isn't just interested in this one woman, but in the stories created by her death and developing around it. She might have read Virginia Woolf as well as James and Conrad. As in Woolf's fictions, Ilse makes the point of view jump from one person to the next. The journalist appears. He's looking for stories like this racy "Underground Murder," because nobody wants to read about the riots in India. There's the tube driver whose train ran over the woman, the policeman interviewing the driver, the man dispatching the replacement buses for the passengers, the mother of the dead woman who tells the press that "Janet was such a happy girl," the psychiatrist who sits in his cream-and-gold decorated office reading about the killing, his secretary, appropriately dressed in cream and gold, who stifles a yawn and puts her pencil into her handbag when her boss tells her that tomorrow he's going to dictate something to her about this, from a scientific psychiatric perspective. In a flashback at the very end of Ilse's story, the young woman appears, walks down the underground stairs, stands next to the thin young man on the platform, waits until she hears the sounds of the incoming train, sees the lights approach, and then Janet, "such a happy girl," in a movement she has thought about a few times before, jumps in front of the train. Nobody pushed her.

* * * * *

Ilse paints stripes onto the awnings of Mediterranean vegetable carts. She squints her eyes. The friend who has given her this job owns a toy store in touristy St. Ives. It's Ilse's assignment to apply color to small wooden soldiers, horses, and these tiny Sicilian market stands. Ilse is notoriously clumsy. Kit is so good with his hands. And he's a painter. So he seems very well qualified for this. But there's the understanding that he needs to dedicate himself fully to his art. His painting seems more important than Ilse's writing.

When she's done with the stripes, she holds a soldier in one hand, the paintbrush in the other. She tenses up. It's incredibly difficult to focus on the tiny soldier's tiny nose and to place an even tinier dot there.

* * * * *

Another writer just got married here in Cornwall, in Lelant, just eight miles away, in December 1946. Her pen name is Jane Fraser. She too puts her career second to her husband's and moves to Scotland with him. He'll take over his parent's textile company. She's going to raise their four kids. When there's time, she will be writing stories, with very limited success. And then, when she's in her mid-sixties, she will get rid of her pseudonym and publish, under her real name, a novel set in Cornwall, among other places; a book the *New York Times* will call "deeply satisfying." Over the course of her life, Rosamunde Pilcher will sell more than sixty million books. In a new millennium, tens of thousands of German tourists will travel to Cornwall each year, drawn by the locations of German TV movies based on the works of the writer formerly known as Jane Fraser. In these adaptations, German actors play romantically inclined Brits. The tourists go to Mevagissey because they've seen "Serpents in Paradise" and they go to Zennor because of "Snowstorm in the Spring."[6]

* * * * *

Ilse and Kit get married in London. It's June 2, 1948. Kit is wearing one of George's suits. Ilse's probably wearing one of her own dresses. On the marriage certificate, the registrar notes that Albert Gordon Barker is the son of George Barker, butler, and his status that of a bachelor. Underneath "rank or profession" the registrar writes "artist." For the daughter of the deceased wine merchant Karl Gross, the registrar records: "Formerly the wife of Geoffrey Pittock-Buss, from whom she obtained a divorce." Under Ilse's "rank or profession," the registrar draws a long dash. That means: none.

* * * * *

Then they're back in Cornwall. Every morning Ilse goes to get a churn of milk from their landlords. The Barkers are always behind with the rent and milk money. Every day the feeling comes afresh that they'll refuse to fill the churn.

Two of Kit's works were exhibited in a gallery in Grosvenor Street, London, and a critic mentioned them in *The Spectator*. That was a success. And he had a two-man show in a book shop in St. Ives. Important people saw that show. Art people trudged up the hill to their home, even George

Dix from New York, gallerist for the Durlacher Brothers. Dix bought two drawings. Then that moment, Kit's moment, was over. What is Ilse doing with her stories? Who is she showing them to? It's unclear.

The farmers here are also poor, almost as poor as the writers and the artists. Their horses and cows are haggard. The soil is stony. The farmers think the bohemians are lazy, but all day and every day the bohemians are occupied with just staying alive. When Ilse and Kit return home, they always pretend to be engaged in deep conversation. That way their landlords will hopefully refrain from interrupting them with questions about the rent.

* * * * *

She'll keep working on the Veronica novel: the woman looking for freedom in Cornwall. Soon Ilse's fiction is going to seem much less experimental than her London tube story. Her works will be tightly structured, plausible, their language precise.

Ilse decides to make Veronica a poet. And this poet will be so lucky – or so tremendously unlucky – to have a very impressive older brother, Everett. Also a poet. A very impressive poet. His lines make people shiver. Veronica's own poetry seems softer, smaller, her images more mundane and the pain addressed by them less significant. Her heart always contracts a little when someone mentions brilliant Everett to her. In these moments, Veronica feels as though her presence isn't enough.

* * * * *

Kit and Ilse are eating potatoes and not much more. They live similarly to most Britons. The country won the war, and the postwar era is austere. The Ministry of Food does something it never did during the war: Bread is now rationed.

Rich people can buy what they want on the black market. Poor people go hungry. In Birmingham a woman sees the royal couple from afar. They're visiting the city. This woman feels that in contrast to her subjects the queen seems a bit too well-fed.[7]

Ilse still doesn't like sardines, but sardines are cheap, so they're a staple, in a batter made from oatmeal, should they have oatmeal. Sometimes they get monkfish, because nobody else wants monkfish, and they eat it even though it's monkfish. Sometimes they "find" a head of cabbage somewhere in a field and they hope nobody's watching. Getting food on credit is impossible here. Ilse tried the butcher's once. Half a pound of sausages. She asked for generosity. No such luck. And there's no credit in the pub either. The Cornwall experiment is over. They can't pay back the money they owe for milk and rent, so the farmer takes their bed instead.

6

New York City

She opens the door to her suite and sees the white roses. She's a professional novelist now, widely read, and she has come to New York to accept a highly prestigious literary prize. The carpets are deep here, and her skyscraper suite is high up.

Jake, her publisher, must have sent the flowers. She removes the pins from her hair. She takes off her gloves. She looks at the card. There it is. Just: "Jake." How romantic. Her husband hasn't sent flowers.

She goes shopping with Jake. It feels good. His greying hair makes him look distinguished. They do look handsome next to each other, as the department store mirrors show. She could imagine being the spoiled young wife of an older, important husband. But when Jake proposes to her at the end of their shopping afternoon, she tells him how sorry she is. In spite of everything that has happened, she still loves her husband. She wants to save her marriage, though she will always feel the warmest affection for Jake.

After numerous cocktail parties, she opens the telegrams congratulating her on her prize. She appreciates every new flower bouquet delivered to her suite. She looks at her photograph in the evening papers. Now her husband has sent a telegram, too, and, separately, her husband's new mistress.

The next day she receives the prize. Her meticulously composed acceptance speech strikes an idealistic tone. She hopes to inspire young people – all of those out there striving for fame and success. And she develops a clear vision for the literature of the future. Then all the cameras flash and the sound of applause rushes over her and she switches from water to champagne. Her name is Frances Siddorn. She's an American writer. She's the heroine of Ilse's second novel: *The Innermost Cage*, published in 1955.

* * * * *

In the winter of 1948/49, it's hard for Ilse to take a shower. Kit's father keeps hiding the key to the boiler. After leaving Cornwall, Kit and Ilse moved in with the Barkers in London. Now they're waiting for their U.S. visa. Ilse was granted a loan by a Jewish aid organization. It was just enough to pay for the transatlantic tickets. They need more money, so she takes work as a typist at the London "Institute of Petroleum," where experts in the British energy sector broaden their horizons. Their secretary would really like to shower according to her own free will.

She lost her first family, her German-Jewish family. Now she belongs to the Irish-English Barkers. Kit's mother spends the entire day on her couch, surrounded by her children, grandchildren, friends, and by the poets and painters George and Kit bring along. First there's tea and then Big Mumma opens the bottle of port. On Sundays the sitting room's particularly crowded, because the pubs don't open until the evening. People wait at the Barkers' until the time has come. To prepare, they count their change and Mother Barker looks into her purse and pushes coins across the table towards them. And then someone says that it's seven and they all set off.

In the pub there are fixed rules, Ilse learns. You can't sit. That would be effete. You're supposed to drink standing up, and while drinking you're expected to voice as many original opinions as you possibly can. Kit's brother excels in this department. Over beers George shouts, for example, that painting is far too easy. Writing poetry? So much more complex! If he, George Barker, though a poet, were to start painting, he'd be a better painter than his painter brother. From. Day. One. The painter brother stands, drinks, and listens.

After the pub closes, they return to the Barkers and there are more drinks and then a lot of singing. The men in the Barker crowd feel very confident about their beautiful voices. They sing "Royal Blackbird" – about the damsel whose blackbird has disappeared and who moans and cries because nobody could ever be as loyal and as courageous as her blackbird. They sing "I Sing of a Maiden," about the mother of the king of kings: "Mother and Maiden / There was never ever one but she." A general rule applies. These men sing about women, but women aren't really supposed to sing. And there's this woman who's neither mother nor maiden and will have to man the typewriter tomorrow at the "Institute of Petroleum." She does wish the Barkers wouldn't sing as much.

When she gets up in the morning, she only sees one family member: Kit's and George's father. He's a butler at Gray's Inn. To his grown-up sons their father is a joke because he's so self-disciplined and serious. Every morning he leaves the Headquarters of Bohemia in a black coat, a bowler hat on his head, and an umbrella under his arm. In the evening Ilse and her father-in-law hide the bread they'll need for breakfast, in some place where the singing hungry drunkards won't be able to find it at night.

*　*　*　*　*

Kit and Ilse leave London in May 1949. Ernst, her cousin from Bingen, has supplied an affidavit for them. He is now Ernest, from New Rochelle, New York. They have immigration visas for the United States. They could stay for the rest of their lives.

Ilse is seasick, for twelve days, and then the Statue of Liberty appears. One thing strikes them in the harbor: In New York, longshoremen can afford voluminous cigars. In England, that's unthinkable. They sublet an apartment from friends, in a dilapidated building on the Lower East Side. In the ashtrays they see long cigarette butts. That is also odd. In impoverished England everyone smokes their fags down to the last tiny bit.

*　*　*　*　*

They need money, and they need it soon. They meet the painter Virginia Admiral. She has separated from her husband Robert De Niro, who's also a painter. Their son, another Robert De Niro, she raises by herself. Little Robert is difficult, perhaps a bit temperamental. But that isn't going to hold him back.

Virginia makes a living as a secretary. She introduces Ilse to her boss. But Ilse doesn't type fast enough. Robert De Niro Sr. makes money painting neckties. It's piecework. Each individual tie painter adds only one or two colors and then moves the tie down to the next painter. The finished products show palm trees, parrots, toucans, monkeys, and the occasional half-naked woman. Kit takes the job.

You can buy bananas in New York, bananas at long last. And in bars here, you're supposed to leave a tip on the counter. It's very hard to get used to that, especially because Kit doesn't paint ties anymore.

On the subway they seem particularly poor. They've come from a country without washing machines, a country where soap is rationed, the island of the dirty raincoat, worn with pride. On the New York subway they see laborers with perfectly clean overalls and office workers with impossibly dazzling white shirts.

In their neighborhood old women approach Ilse on the street. They talk to her in Yiddish, Polish, Lithuanian. Possibly, she can only guess, they want to find out whether she's a long-lost East European relative.

Then they have to move out of their first apartment and find a place in Harlem. Another language: now they're surrounded by Puerto Rican Spanish. People say that their next-door neighbor is a gangster and that he might be hiding a dead body in his refrigerator. He does have a refrigerator.

Quickly they learn what it means to live in Harlem. On one occasion, Kit loses his wallet in the street. It's a tragedy to them; there was a ten-dollar bill in that wallet. A few weeks later they receive a letter. Someone in Harlem found the wallet and handed it in to the police and then someone contacted the English address found in there and then Kensington got in touch with Harlem and Harlem with the Barkers. They go to the station to pick up the wallet and find the ten-dollar bill inside and they're not quite as poor as they had thought.

* * * * *

How fascinating it is to meet the New York painters. Or how fascinating it would be if the New York painters were a bit different. Ilse Barker observes that New York painters are interested in one thing only: New York painters. Literature doesn't exist for them. Nor does music. Nor does European art. And whereas in England, artists help each other – it's normal "to put in a good word" – here everyone's uninteresting unless they're on the fast track to success.

So many things are different in New York then. But there's one thing that's exactly the same. Women are expected to take on day jobs so their male partners will have enough time to focus on their art. If these women happen to be artists themselves, few people take notice. Lee Krasner, Jackson Pollock's partner, is a stupendous painter. Since Pollock has turned into a media star, she's become a nonentity. It's similar with the de Koonings: Elaine receives only scant attention, Willem's officially a Great Artist. Gestural and athletic, the new trend in painting, abstract expressionism, comes across as a bodily art form: It seems clear to everyone who has a say here – in other words: men – that these pieces could only be produced by men. And the paintings are getting bigger and bigger.[1]

On workdays Ilse puts on one of her two dresses and walks to the subway. Kit stays home to dedicate himself to his art. Ilse works in advertising now, in a windowless open-plan office in Midtown. Her department is called "Media Typing." She types the names of cities, dates, newspapers, and radio stations. She types broadcasting schedules for cigarette and detergent commercials, for soap operas. The typewriters are not electric and very clunky. The bosses watch Ilse and the other typists from their little cubicles. These cubicles don't have windows either. Only the bosses' bosses see the light of day.

Her fellow typists are from the Bronx or Queens. On every desk there's a glass pane, and each typist places photos below the glass. On the other desks Ilse sees pictures of boyfriends. Her co-workers insist, however, that of course they haven't lost their virginity yet. Below the glass next to Ilse's typewriter, she put a poem by Gerard Manley Hopkins: "No Worst, There is None." It explores the human spirit and the mountains rising up within and frightening cliffs and the fact that death ends every life and that "each day dies with sleep."

The other typists wear something different every day. Everything's freshly laundered. The women are perfectly nice, but they do ask Ilse why she doesn't have more clothes to choose from.

Ilse makes forty-five dollars a week. Twenty-one of those dollars pay their rent. That doesn't leave much. Ilse needs subway tokens. Kit needs paint and canvas and paintbrushes. He paints fish and the sea, and he is terribly homesick for England. Their idea of a luxurious day consists of getting one sandwich and one milkshake at Woolworth's and dividing both between them. Pawnbrokers' shops are very impressive in New York. Bright lights, long counters. Every now and again Ilse walks inside and leaves without her mother's emerald ring.

When they go to the Museum of Modern Art, they only get one ticket. That's how they save money. Ilse waits in the lobby until Kit comes back out. Then they go for a walk, and he tells her about all the interesting avantgarde art he saw.

✶ ✶ ✶ ✶ ✶

The woman named Catherine Talbot doesn't have a minute to spare. All she wants to do is read and write, but she must do what the bishop tells her to do. She can't refuse, because her father died before she was born, in 1721, and the bishop was so generous as to take her mother and her in. Because she's forever indebted to him, she has to accompany the bishop on visits and write letters for him, and because that keeps her so busy there's almost no time at all for her own literary ambitions. Catherine Talbot ranks as one of the most prominent female intellectuals of the eighteenth century.[2] Ilse Barker's new pen name: Kathrine Talbot.

* * * * *

In a short story she writes in New York, Ilse Barker/Kathrine Talbot imagines a male author who could not be more privileged. The great Richard Donnington resides in an elegant house by a river. His wife, Bella, much younger than he, is so beautiful and yet so unassuming, so delicate and small and charming and shy. And because Bella's so pretty she sits by the window for Richard Donnington. When he's at his desk, working, he enjoys seeing his young wife whenever he looks up from a manuscript. Her quiet presence inspires him; it helps him attain and hold on to literary greatness. Things could just stay the way they are, but then one day, delicate Bella, would you believe it, asks her husband if perhaps she might also work a little while sitting by the window. It does make the great writer smile that his wife would use the verb "work" in this context. But he doesn't object. And that's something he'll live to regret.

* * * * *

Ilse and Kit go to the bars in the Village. They meet Clem. He isn't particularly attractive, but kind of sexy, and a very good dancer. Ilse dances with Clem when the jukebox is playing. These dances Kit doesn't seem to mind, but he probably doesn't share Clem's opinion that from this point on in human history, only American art will count. Clement "Clem" Greenberg is the most important art critic in the United States – and from now on this means: the most important in the world.

Jimmy Ernst, Max Ernst's son, invites them to a party in his apartment. He has hired a barkeeper for the event. Ilse is impressed. Jimmy was born in Cologne. His real name: Hans-Ulrich. His mother, Luise Straus-Ernst, was killed in Auschwitz.[3] Ilse notes that Jimmy seems to be the only one in this circle who doesn't believe that the world revolves around New York.

* * * * *

The writer Kathrine Talbot needs to write. She could find time on Sundays. But on Saturdays they get home very late from the bars and every Sunday morning the neighbor who might be a gangster plays his favorite song, "Joltin' Joe DiMaggio," and he plays it again and again, at the highest possible volume. The track praises the best baseball player of their time. What the neighbor doesn't realize is that the bohemians next door had a really short night's sleep, and that there's an author here who really needs to focus because on Monday morning she has to go back to "Media Typing."

Kathrine Talbot sends short stories to magazines and gets rejection letters. The letters belong to the better category of rejections. Editors tell her that the story she sent didn't quite fit – and that they would really like to see something else she has written.

In the Sunday paper they read about this idyllic place where painters and authors, sculptors and composers can spend time to work on their projects. They live rent-free. They get free food. And then they can be creative in peace. Kit and Ilse could apply. It would mean salvation. A dream. Paradise. But it is extremely unlikely that this unbelievable colony would accept both of them at the same time.

* * * * *

She has family here in New York. For the first time in a long while, cousins live close to her, uncles and aunts. These Jews from Bingen made it. They survived.

She isn't enthusiastic about spending time with them. And her relatives aren't so keen either – because Kit and Ilse haven't achieved much. Cousin Ernest arrived in New York and founded a successful picture agency. Black Star represents some of the best photojournalists of the era.[4] Ilse's aunt Alice applied for her very first job at the age of forty-five and now commutes to Manhattan every day and takes human bones, joints, and skulls out of boxes. These she assembles into skeletons that will help teach future physicians.

One cousin holds the position of sommelier on the Queen Mary. Another leads the Electricity Department at Brazil's National Institute of Technology. Cousin Willy in England, Ilse hears, passed his exam. His trademark method, insulin shock therapy, will seem somewhat brutal in the near future. But for now he's a top-notch psychiatrist.[5] In the case of the Barkers, however, the situation is as follows: Kit doesn't make any money and Ilse types.

* * * * *

She keeps working on celebrated male geniuses. After destroying Richard Donnington she writes a story about the sudden silence of a brilliant composer. "Death in the Pyrenees" explores his downfall and mysterious end, perhaps by drinking himself to death in New York, perhaps while helping Jewish refugees cross the border between France and Spain. She's a Jewish refugee too, but in her story the migrants seem completely insignificant. This author is only interested in the great artist: in his monumentality and in his end.

* * * * *

Ilse's office mates in "Media Typing" give her farewell presents. The package contains typing paper, paper clips and a range of other utensils they stole from the office. Kit and Ilse have really done it. They both have been granted fellowships at Yaddo, the artists' colony in Saratoga Springs.

They go 180 miles north. There are oil paintings on the walls and Tiffany lamps everywhere. The Barkers have a gigantic bathroom to themselves. Ilse's free here. They don't have to clean, and they don't have to cook. In the Barker household, Kit neither cleans nor cooks, so this is a gift only to her. Yaddo's creative guests always have breakfast together and then everybody receives their lunch and goes off to work. After a few hours, they have lunch in the rose garden or by one of the Yaddo lakes. Then a few more hours, and then the working day is over and dinner brings inspiring conversation.

Ilse takes a look at the studio reserved for her and her alone. It is all in white: the desk, the chair, the marble bust of a woman who'll be looking over her shoulder as she writes. If she writes. She notices that Kit can't cope

here. The group. His shyness. Too many people. For two days, she monitors
how things are going for him. Then she walks into the white studio and sits
down by herself. As Virginia Woolf writes: "A woman must have money
and a room of her own if she is to write fiction."[6] Ilse writes her Cornwall
novel: *Fire in the Sun*.

* * * * *

Her fiction, inspired by Henry James, illuminates the problems of sensitive,
cultivated, and affluent people. In Kathrine Talbot's Cornwall, nobody has
holes in their Wellingtons. Nobody goes hungry. Nobody is looking for the
outhouse in the fog. Though World War Two has only just ended in her
novel, none of her protagonists seems traumatized by wartime experiences.
Poet Veronica might be frustrated by the insignificance of her literary
production, but an inheritance soothes her pain. And she owns a flat in
London. The book explores love and artistic ambitions and the charisma
of a poet who confounds far too many sensitive people. Ilse writes a third
of the novel. That's enough to sell it to a publishing house. One of the big
New York presses – Putnam's – buys her work. Now all she needs to do is
finish it.

* * * * *

They return from Yaddo, back to Harlem, and Ilse once again finds herself
sitting behind her desk in Midtown. It seems that Putnam's didn't pay her
much of an advance. Her cousin Ernst/Ernest sometimes lends her money.
Sometimes he takes her out to lunch. She looks at the poem next to the
typewriter. "No Worst, There is None." Kit stays home to paint. He's still
just some English artist nobody has ever heard of.

And then Cousin Ernest realizes that he knows this artist Hans Möller,
now Moller. Moller in turn knows the art collector couple Fred and Florence
Olson. So one day Ilse and Kit Barker are invited to the apartment of Helen
and Hans Moller, for a dinner with the Olsons, who happen to be in town,
staying at the Waldorf-Astoria. This is the opportunity for Kit to get to
know affluent collectors. For once he can be more than George's sibling.
And of course, over dinner Helen Moller tells Florence Olson that Kit is the

famous George Barker's younger brother – and isn't that the poet Florence loved so much? Florence is so enthusiastic that she starts reciting George's sonnet "To My Mother." She knows it by heart. The woman "most near, most dear, most loved, and most far," the woman "huge as Asia." The brass band, the little dog, the gin-drinking, courageous mother never looking up at German bombers, taking care of every injured bird.

Kit survives this recitation. And apparently the Olsons see something in them. A few weeks later they invite Kit and Ilse for drinks at the Waldorf and then to dinner at a sophisticated French place, and then the Olsons, who own Picassos and Pollocks and Klees and Mirós, will also buy Kit Barker's paintings. For their private residence. For one of their private residences.

* * * * *

On October 6, 1950, twelve men enter a German courtroom. They stand trial for "crimes against humanity," committed on November 9 and November 10, 1938, when mobs destroyed both synagogues of Bingen and looted Jewish shops and homes. They attacked the homes of the wine merchants Roos and Hausmann, and the teacher Weiss, the Münzener's discount shop in Kapuzinerstraße, and the butcher's in Amtsstraße. The group of defendants consists of a vineyard worker, a musician, a bank clerk, an agricultural helper, a retired customs official, a truck driver, a roofer, a brick layer, a mechanic, a senior forestry clerk, a horticultural inspector, and a railway official. Four of these men are acquitted immediately. Eight of them are more complex cases.

The bank clerk admits to having thrown clothes from the reform synagogue onto the street. The roofer states that he did indeed climb a ladder to destroy the Star of David and the Tablets of the Law on the synagogue's front wall. He says the mayor of Bingen had told him to do so. The horticultural inspector says that he had found himself close to the synagogue at some point that night, but that he'd gone home in the exact moment when the acts of destruction began.

The judge listens to the men and to additional testimonies. The trial has lasted for just a few hours and then it ends because all the charges are dropped. The year 1938, the judge explains, had seen "a certain mass psychosis." The actions in question had been ordered by the "highest authorities." And all the events had happened such a long time ago. "The need for atonement and retribution," the judge declares, "is no longer especially pronounced."[7]

⋆ ⋆ ⋆ ⋆ ⋆

In November 1950, Ilse and Kit return to Yaddo. This time they have their own little house. It's even quieter now and even more idyllic. There are fewer people around and the ones that did come play a lot more table tennis than in the summer. Novelist Katherine Anne Porter is a sore loser.[8]

Ilse writes the second third of the Cornwall novel and then the final third. Everything revolves around Veronica, the poet, and Everett, the brilliant brother overshadowing her. Veronica's fiancé, a painter, works on a double portrait of Veronica and Everett. Initially, the sister is in the foreground and her brother in the background. The fiancé paints and paints, starts to wonder whether the brother might not belong in front and the sister in the back, and then reaches for a bottle of turpentine.

Apparently Yaddo inspired Ilse to move her protagonist to an artist's colony. "Trevartha:" her name for the creative paradise of Cornwall. There the unbelievably charismatic Everett not only unhitches Veronica's fiancé from her, but also two other men who were greatly interested in her before rapidly falling for her wonderful brother. From then on Veronica feels painfully alone.

⋆ ⋆ ⋆ ⋆ ⋆

In this Yaddo winter, Ilse meets Elizabeth Bishop. She's an important poet with a drinking problem. A perfectionist, compulsively shy. Behind Bishop lies a failed relationship with a millionaire heiress and then another love and another break-up. She's almost forty now, and she has published one book of poems. It received an important literary prize, but it's still only one book. It's critical that she produce another one shortly. And she just needs a few more poems. Bishop's writer's block kicked in at the exact moment when she realized that a few more poems were all she needed.

Kit Barker and Elizabeth Bishop talk a great deal in Yaddo. They both have asthma, they're both far too coy. He is an artist who keeps painting fish, and Bishop's only book so far – and who knows whether "so far" is really accurate – contains a very long poem portraying a very ugly fish. The poem describes the fish with all its flaws. There are five broken hooks in its mouth and lice all over its body. "And I let the fish go." That's the last line.

Kit must have said something very helpful to Elizabeth Bishop. Years later she will thank him for it. Whatever it was he suggested, one day Bishop trudges through the Yaddo snow and walks into Ilse's and Kit's cabin. She's holding a page in her hand. A new poem. The blockade is over.

Ilse Barker and Elizabeth Bishop are passionate letter writers. After saying goodbye in Yaddo they will correspond for decades, across North America, across the Atlantic, from the Northern to the Southern Hemisphere. They will send each other the most intimate, beautiful, spectacular letters, of which Ilse Barker will keep more than two hundred and Elizabeth Bishop fewer than twenty.[9]

* * * * *

At the end of the Cornwall novel, its author must find something that lonely Veronica could do. Everett and his men go for walks a lot. Veronica remains behind. And novelist Kathrine Talbot chooses the most dramatic solution. Returning from one of their hikes, the men climb up the last hill before Trevartha and come down the hill on the other side and because the sun is in their eyes, they don't really comprehend what they're seeing. The flames are almost invisible – as invisible as Veronica has become to these men. Then the men make out the smoke. Veronica has set fire to the artist's paradise. The men start running. They're probably not fast enough.

* * * * *

And then, in snowy Yaddo, Ilse talks to handsome Calvin Kentfield. Maybe, with hindsight, it would have been better if she hadn't.

Like her, Calvin has sold his first novel to a publisher. He was once a seaman in the South Pacific, with the U.S. Merchant Marine. Then he went back to college, in Iowa, pretty far from any sort of ocean. But he turned his years at sea into his literary debut.

Ilse tells Calvin that she'd be happy to type up the final chapter of his novel. In exchange, Calvin will read her Cornwall manuscript. Sitting at the typewriter, she notices the enormous weaknesses in Calvin's writing. How improvised the language seems, how sloppy the structure. And the very premise: Calvin Kentfield spent time in the South Seas and here he writes about someone who spent time in the South Seas. That, Ilse finds, is not how literature works.

She spent time in Cornwall and then she wrote a Cornwall novel. But she insists that the central theme of that work bears no relation to her actual life. As a fourteen-year-old, Ilse heard a lecture that she, a Jewish girl, was a lower lifeform; she escaped and got deported and survived the "Full Moon" and the "Baby Blitz" and the V-1 and the V-2 and she opened a letter at the breakfast table that said her parents had been killed, in the German camps, and which ended with the words "Yours sincerely, Victor Lehmann." Vividly she recalls the last time she saw her parents: her father's last wave, the hat her mother wore that summer, the final embrace. But she won't write about these things. Not for a very long time. She says that literature shouldn't have more than an indirect connection to a lived life. You experience things and these experiences sink into the unconscious, and from your unconscious, fiction rises to the surface.

She hands the typed pages to her dashing fellow novelist and at first she can't summon the courage to tell him what she thinks. In his creative career, Calvin Kentfield will publish two short story collections about his life at sea, a novel titled *All Men Are Seamen*, a nonfiction book about the Pacific Coast and an autobiographical account titled *Memoirs of a Seaman in the Merchant Marine*.[10] Calvin informs her that he disliked her novel. Which makes it possible for Ilse to tell him what she really thought. Both appalled, they part ways.

Ilse Gross, in Bingen, thirteen years old (1934).

Ilse Gross, enemy alien. Internment ID card (1940). Source: Manx National Heritage.

Ilse Gross and her father, Karl Gross (1930s).

Grape harvest, Bingen, around 1930. First row, third from right: Ilse Gross.

Wedding photograph: Ilse and
Geoffrey Pittock-Buss (1941).

Ilse Pittock-Buss (c. 1946)

Reception photograph, Ilse and Kit Barker's wedding (1948).

Ilse and Kit, late 1940s.

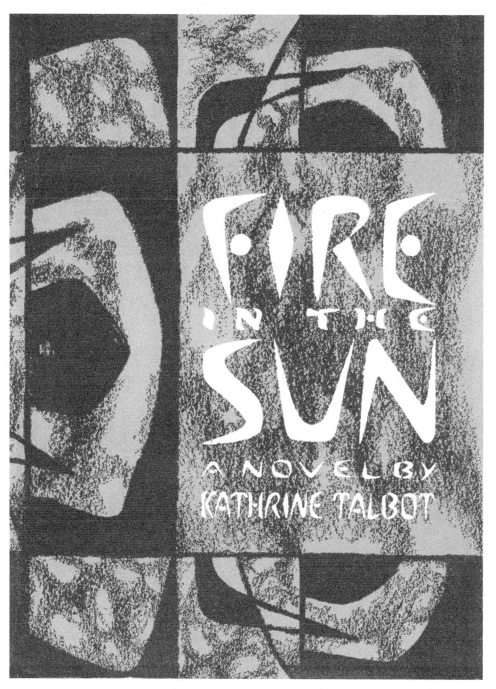

Cover, Kathrine Talbot: *Fire in the Sun* (1952).

The
Innermost Cage

A Novel by
Kathrine Talbot

Cover, Kathrine Talbot: *The Innermost Cage* (1955).

RETURN

A NOVEL
by
Kathrine
Talbot

published by Faber and Faber

Cover, Kathrine Talbot: *Return* (1959).

Bexley Hill (c. 1960).

Ilse and cat Hepplewhite (1960s).

Ilse and Tom (1964).

Ilse (1990).

A Bingen classroom. Ilse Gross: third row, first from the left (c. 1930).

Ilse Gross and her mother, Agnes Gross (Switzerland, 1938).

7

Wood

The young man cleaning the house is planning a career as a mortician. At this point, he's a servant to the living – and Ilse and Kit are among them. They took a Greyhound out West. And they now live with the Olsons in Alton, Illinois, a suburb of St. Louis. They're immersed in an American upper-class existence, and that includes African American domestics: the cook in her uniform, always neatly pressed, and the male servant. Ilse finds that he talks about undertaking in fascinating detail. Fred and Florence Olson call him their "house boy."

Above the Olson's fireplace is a Hans Hofmann painting with a beautiful stripe in magenta. Next to the Hofmann there's a Picasso: a bowl of cherries. Not far away, on the floor, lies a Miró rug. A Motherwell painting decorates the hallway. On a wall in Ilse and Kit's bedroom hangs Paul Klee's "Child with a Flower," and, right over their bed, a watercolor by Jackson Pollock. In the evenings neither the cook nor the "house boy" fix cocktails: Fred Olson makes them himself. During the day, at the local arts supply store, Kit is welcome to select as many brushes, as much paint, and as much canvas as he wants. Fred picks up the bills.

* * * * *

They move on to California, via Taos, New Mexico. In San Francisco they find a small apartment, in Hayes Street, in a dilapidated house. They share their bathroom with a few older men. These men aren't in great condition either. Here, in the spring of 1952, Ilse reads the reviews of her first novel.

In the *New York Times*, critic Robert Raynolds seems annoyed. He sees her protagonists as a bunch of "spiritual thieves." These are people, Raynolds writes, that are trying to "batten" their "childish egos" on one another. And he's not at all happy with the negative treatment *Fire in the Sun* gives to the only woman protagonist who's wishing for a "home" and a "family." In contrast, the *News* in Savannah, Georgia, expresses a sense of relief. While the paper sees "Freudian situations" in her novel, it doesn't categorize it as "extremely abnormal." In Louisville, Kentucky, the *Courier-Journal* calls Kathrine Talbot a talented author. All in all, however, since "perverted values" will always lead to "perverted art," the review advises against reading her work.

George Barker writes from England. He sends his congratulations on *Fire in the Sun*. He notes that there's not enough action for his taste and recommends that Ilse read André Gide. He'd love to write more often, he says. But he's so broke, he can't afford airmail stamps.

* * * * *

She could see as her rival Daphne du Maurier, whose novel *My Cousin Rachel* is also set in Cornwall, and right now, in 1952, tops the American bestseller lists. In du Maurier's book, if someone happens to be standing over a grave, he will certainly swear to avenge the person lying in the ground beneath. A dubious Italian will surely turn out to be really good at heart. And a structurally unsound bridge will collapse – an absolute coincidence – while the heroine is walking across it.

In Kathrine Talbot's novel, no bridges crumble. A house burns. But no oaths are sworn over graves. She isn't fond of melodrama. To her, literature is a field for psychological studies. In 1945, on the banks of the Wye, she read the new Henry Green and she owes much to *Loving*. She wants to create a specific, carefully drawn world. In Green, everything's set in this country house in Ireland; in her novel, it's this one pocket of Cornwall. In such a narrowly defined terrain, you study the emotions of protagonists colliding with each other, and that fills the novel with energy.

In Green's *Loving*, however, all the characters have things in common, no matter how differently they feel and love. They all fear a German invasion of Ireland, they're shocked by German bombs falling on London, and they're afraid of an IRA attack. In Kathrine Talbot's work there's no historical crisis, only creativity and love – and even then, not quite as much love as in Daphne du Maurier. For some readers, that might not be enough.

Kit is now teaching at the California School of Fine Arts. That brings lots of prestige and very little money. As *Fire in the Sun* doesn't turn into a bestseller and because that's the way things always work with them, the woman some know as Kathrine Talbot again looks for a job as a typist. She's hired by IBM.

Her new employer is just about to launch the "701," an early form of the personal computer.[1] They hand the company songbook to Ilse. It contains three songs: "March on with IBM," "Hail to the IBM," and "Ever Onward," which concludes in the lines: "Once or twice then sing again / For the Ever-Onward IBM." The songs praise the company's founder T.J. Watson, whose name should live forever, and the company's fame, which reaches across all the seven seas.

Fifty years later, an investigative journalist, the son of Holocaust survivors, will research IBM's history in detail. He will show how the company's punch card technology, used by the Nazis, helped to register, persecute, and ultimately murder the European Jews.[2]

* * * * *

Ilse's picture appears in the *Saturday Review of Literature*. Under her photograph she sees the name "Kathrine Talbot" and two additional words: "intuitive brilliance." Critic Pamela Taylor praises the novelist's extra-ordinary taste, her work's efficiency, its honesty, and the astounding way in which it presents a sensitive and highly emotional woman. Patty Scratch, writing for the *Hollywood Citizen*, calls *Fire in the Sun* an "excellent psychological novel." The *New York Daily News* lauds its tension and power, building ever so slowly. The *Oakland Tribune* declares Kathrine Talbot's work to be "strongly poetic." In Hartford, Connecticut, the *Times* calls her an "overpowering 'mood' writer."

* * * * *

You find so much wood in the United States. There's so little of it in England. Here you walk around somewhere and suddenly you chance upon an empty wooden house. It may have been visited by skunks, but it consists of solid beams and boards and still nobody lives in it. In England people live in basements, they sleep on the floor, they share a single room with their children, parents, and in-laws. Everyone needs wood over there. Kit and Ilse are strolling along the beach, somewhere near San Francisco, and they see tree trunks, branches, planks. Ilse bows down, picks up a board, then another one, and another one, as if she could send the wood to England.

Maybe it's not the right time for "'mood' writers." Even the positive reviews
don't bring lasting success. The most important American novels of this
time are based on their authors' real experiences. Most of them are men.
James Jones was a soldier in the 27th Infantry and his bestselling *From Here
to Eternity* turned real battles into fiction. Herman Wouk combed the
Pacific on minesweeping missions and transformed that into *The Caine
Mutiny*. These paths aren't open to Kathrine Talbot.

And the great modernists still dominate the literary scene. There are
worlds which only they seem to understand. William Faulkner wins the
National Book Award in 1951: He's the towering authority on the violently
idyllic American South. John Steinbeck, author of *East of Eden*, is the expert
on the West. And Ernest Hemingway you see in the magazines, first holding
giant fish he caught, and then an even bigger trophy, the Pulitzer for *The
Old Man and the Sea*. America trusts Hemingway when it comes to deep-
sea fishing.[3] By contrast, nobody knows Kathrine Talbot, and not very many
people buy her book.

* * * * *

She quits at IBM. In the summer of 1952, they return to Illinois. Fred and
Florence have gone away for a while, and Kit and Ilse play rummy with
Grandpa Olson. He tells stories. They listen. They're living in a millionaire's
mansion, with servants, but they're as good as bankrupt. They wait for
rummy time to end and borrow the Olson's Cadillac and a few beers from
the house bar and then they drive to the Mississippi and sit and look at the
river.

Kit's still homesick for England. It's Ilse's job, however, to write the
weekly letter to his mother. She also corresponds with solicitor Lehmann
in London. Their letters concern reparation payments. The Federal
Republic of Germany needs more information from her.

The novelist Kathrine Talbot has signed a contract for a new novel. But
she's unhappy with her ideas. She can't find a beginning. Kit, in contrast, is
busy painting. He's experimenting with abstraction. One of his new paintings
is called "Echoes of the Clavichord," another one: "Variations on a Heraldic
Element." He thought of a simpler title for "Woman with a Headache."

Then Fred and Florence come back and busy themselves with the plans
for their new house. The sketches cover the dinner table. These, too, look
like abstract art. The Olsons' architect, Tony Smith, has planned a

modernist masterpiece on Long Island Sound, a building offering plenty of room for paintings and sculptures. Yes, there's going to be enough space for the Henry Moore. The main building bends around the swimming pool like an open hand. And the sea is right outside the picture windows. This house captivates Ilse's imagination. It won't let go.

* * * * *

"Write what you know." Soon everyone's going to use that line. Fiction, people now say, should emerge from one's own experiences. According to a new American concept, creative writing can be taught at universities. In classrooms future authors await instruction. Many of them used to be soldiers. What could they write about? Something they know.[4]

"Write what you know." Kathrine Talbot could start a story with the cantor at one of Bingen's synagogues – and how this cantor touched his face with his hand because he wasn't sure what to say. She was there. It wouldn't really be the cantor's story, though, but rather the story of this textile shop in Bingen. Everyone knew it. It was right on the market square. In 1935 the shop owner was sent to prison. He was Jewish and accused of molesting one of his "Aryan" saleswomen. The shop owner's daughter was a small, blonde, pretty girl, always happy, and her birthday parties, so the other girls thought, were the best because they were held in the clothes shop where first coffee and cake were served at a long table and then everyone played hide and seek between all the dresses and hats and coats and left at the end of the day with a balloon and more than enough glittering ribbons. And then one day the Jewish girls of Bingen, all a few years older now, were sitting in the room upstairs in the synagogue, and Hebrew class was held by the cantor, and then someone called him out of the room. The girls all chatted wildly until he came back in. The cantor turned to that little, blonde, constantly happy girl and said she should probably go home. Which she did. Then nobody said anything for a long time until the cantor's hand moved up to his face. He said: "Her mother needs her at home." Her father, the textile shop owner, had committed suicide in his prison cell.

In her new novel, Kathrine Talbot writes about a married couple: an architect and a novelist. He has built a magnificent house for her. It couldn't be more magnificent. They also have a magnificent marriage. Maybe. The architect wants to move on, build somewhere else, a new house, right on the coast, whereas the novelist would like to stay where they are. She has her reasons why she doesn't enjoy the sea. However wonderful, widely read and prizewinning the literary works of this author, Frances Siddorn, there's something deeply flawed about her real-life idea to invite an attractive young woman as a long-term guest to the perfect house and to leave that woman alone with her restless husband.

Kathrine Talbot's *The Innermost Cage*, published by a chronically underfinanced writer, presents fur coat-wearing, cocktail-sipping protagonists. They do have enough wood at their disposal. And once again, the catastrophes of the 20th century are invisible in her book. Kathrine Talbot portrays the two servants of the perfect couple as traumatized Europeans. But she gives no detail as to what they experienced. The plot foregrounds infidelity and not much more.

Then again, elegant Frances Siddorn does have extremely painful memories. As it turns out, she is the child survivor of a shipwreck. She and her parents drifted across the Pacific in a lifeboat, and she looked at the dry lips of her parents and received the last drops of water that her father and mother saved for her. Her parents died of thirst and their daughter turned into a celebrated novelist.

✶ ✶ ✶ ✶ ✶

Kathrine Talbot now writes literary criticism, for the *St. Louis Post-Dispatch*. She reviews the novel of a young Belgian author, Françoise Mallet, who has a fifteen-year-old girl start an affair with her father's mistress. French intellectuals loved the book. Of course they did. Critic Kathrine Talbot seems disappointed. She sees psychologically flat fiction, no literary qualities. She's a bit more forgiving towards Eleanor Lothrop's novel about three unhappy women in New York. She does stress, though, that Lothrop's *Sing for your Supper* reads like a mixture of literature and academic scholarship. In Kathrine Talbot's dictionary, that's not a compliment.

✶ ✶ ✶ ✶ ✶

After leaving the Olsons, Ilse and Kit return to Yaddo, for the third and final time. But they're not going to spend time with Elizabeth Bishop. While on vacation in Brazil, Bishop met a woman. The perfect woman. Bishop now lives with her, in Brazil, in a house where she's surrounded by mice, moths, and bats. She's never been happier in her life. Bishop let two Brazilians borrow Ilse's first novel. She writes that one of them didn't understand it and that the smarter of the two liked it. There are a lot of unattractive people in Brazil, Bishop says. She finds the poor people in particular rather ugly, though she allows for a few Afro-Brazilian exceptions. She begs the Barkers to stay in touch. "I hate to keep losing people," Bishop writes. Are the Barkers really going to return to London? If so, Bishop would like them to send her some stationery, blue, if at all possible, from Smythson, 54 New Bond Street, in Mayfair. 200-300 sheets and 150 envelopes would be wonderful.

*   *   *   *   *

Kathrine Talbot's *The Innermost Cage* will appear in 1955. If it weren't for the *New York Times,* her second book could turn into a flawless success. Other papers will praise her novel: its psychological exactitude, its tight plotting, the refined style. And the most important North American newspaper will also call her prose "precise" and "poetic." But the review's headline is impossible to overlook. It reads: "Shipwrecked Novelist." That has an awful double meaning and it's even more awful because it appears in the *New York Times.*

The *Times* critic Olga Owens takes issue with the novel's final scene. It shows Frances Siddorn walking down from her perfect house across her perfect estate to her perfect private pond. She climbs into a little boat and starts rowing, despite her fear of water, her childhood trauma, and her survivor guilt. And of course, this little boat ride on the pond brings Frances back to her memories of the murderous ocean, the lifeboat, and her parents dying of thirst before her very eyes. And that irks Olga Owens. Is this really how a woman would handle this tragedy? In a little rowboat on a pond? With such a horrible experience on the other end of the metaphor? Owens declares the scene "silly" and "forced." Her overall rating: "shipwreck."

Maybe Ilse Barker realizes that Olga Owens is right. The parents' agony and the little boat simply don't connect. The two scenes seem ridiculous in comparison. And this is because certain stories she can't tell. Which is why she must tell surrogate stories instead. There's everyday life in 1950s America and cocktails and plush hotel suites and then there's the destruction of the European Jews, about which she, the author Kathrine Talbot, keeps silent, probably because a certain 20th-century individual named Ilse Barker is unwilling or unable to explore these unimaginable events, and maybe also because in these times very few people want to hear such stories, and maybe because Ilse Barker invented "Kathrine Talbot," an English "'mood' writer" with "intuitive brilliance" who can't suddenly turn German-Jewish history into her theme. At some point, many years later, she will be able to write about her family's true story. But not yet. And so Kathrine Talbot needs to invent other images, other scenes. The pain is real, and she found a place for it in the novel. Hence the little boat. Hence the pond. Clearly she wanted to hide the actual origin of that pain away, though, and Olga Owens noticed. And now the readers of the *New York Times* know, too. This is surely going to hurt Ilse Barker. Though that kind of pain may also seem ridiculous in comparison.

8

Sussex

By late 1952, Kit and Ilse have returned to London. Three and a half years have passed and nettles are growing in the gaps left by German bombs. Food is still rationed. Father Barker's still hiding the key to the boiler.

Ilse would like to live in the country. Right now they aren't completely broke. Kit has sold a few paintings, Ilse her second novel. They have two hundred pounds to their name. For fifty pounds they buy a twenty-year-old Austin and drive it around Kent and Sussex, looking for a house they could buy.

The Gills, friends of George's, live in a place you could call a château. There's a Jaguar out front, paintings of maritime battles inside, and at the back a generous lawn. David Gill tells Kit and Ilse about an empty little house close-by, on Bexley Hill. It's been there since 1565. They drive up the hill, get out of the car, duck their heads to cross the threshold and keep them ducked. For 16th century human beings, the ceilings were probably high enough. The house doesn't have electricity, nor running water, and the privy can be found under a yew tree. It's exactly what they were looking for. But there's no way they can afford it.

* * * * *

In Bingen on the Rhine, Karl and Agnes Gross always kept their libretti in a cabinet underneath the bookshelves. When they listened to operas on the radio, they followed the texts, spread out in front of them across their knees. They always had two copies, one for her father and one for her mother, so they could listen and read at the same time. Her mother's favorite opera was *Aida*, her father's: *Cavalleria Rusticana*.

In 1953, the year she turns thirty-two, Ilse learns that an eyewitness has written to her relatives, telling them that Karl Gross worked as a stretcher bearer in Theresienstadt. That her father was always optimistic or said he was. That he never complained. In the autumn of 1943, he exchanged his warm winter coat for a loaf of bread. He wanted the bread for his hungry wife. The eyewitness related that her mother had lost her mind. She wandered through the camp, begging other inmates for coins. She told them she needed the money so she could follow her daughter to England. Karl Gross died of malnourishment in Theresienstadt. Agnes Gross was deported to Auschwitz and killed there.

✴ ✴ ✴ ✴ ✴

The country around the cottage on Bexley Hill belongs to the Viscount Cowdray. On his mother's side, he is related to Winston Churchill. He lost his left arm at Dunkirk. In the late 20th century only fourteen Brits will be wealthier than the third Viscount Cowdray.[1]

The Gills lend the Barkers the additional money they need. The house is surrounded by trees – wild, ancient woods – and these woods will be chopped down by the Viscount at some point and then the Barkers are certainly going to miss them, even though they'll be able to enjoy a wonderful new view from Bexley Hill. Then a new forest will grow, and the view will be a little less magnificent and the forest not nearly as wild as the one before. All of this they will experience there.

✴ ✴ ✴ ✴ ✴

Elizabeth Bishop writes from Brazil. Because of the architect Lota de Macedo Soares, she has turned her South American vacation into an indefinite stay. People around her tell her that Lota is the smartest woman in the whole of Brazil. Bishop is sure she has found the love of her life.

Every few weeks, Bishop and the Barkers exchange long letters. The letters explore toothaches, pets, shingles. How Brazilians make coffee. The differences between punctuation in American English and in British English. Bishop discusses art with Kit and literature with Ilse. Bishop raises the question of whether to buy a Jaguar or a Mercedes-Benz. The Barkers note that stamps for letters to Brazil are really quite expensive. In the autumn Ilse writes a sad letter about writing, problems with writing, and the lack of appreciation that her work receives. Bishop responds saying how much she had always loved the Barkers' honesty and how they never used other people in the way New Yorkers did. Then she talks about her own frustrations as a writer and how at certain random points things did work out and how the next day, reading what she wrote the day before, she always wonders how in the world she could have written something that trite.

* * * * *

His name is Leslie and he's talking about mice. He was still called Lothar when he got on a train in Berlin in 1938, thirteen years old, a child of the Kindertransport. Now, fifteen years later, he's giving a lecture in London. To the members of the British Society for Experimental Biology, he shows pictures of white mice with a few brown flecks. Leslie explains how his research group managed to graft onto the bodies of these mice the skin of other types of mice.

His sister could have come along to England. But she might have just fallen in love with someone, so she decided to stay. His parents and sister were deported to Riga. In the woods of Rumbula, they were shot. Only after 1989 will Leslie find out more about the exact circumstances.

Seven years after this London lecture, Leslie's supervisor will receive the Nobel Prize for Medicine and share the prize money with Leslie and another colleague. Late in his life, Leslie Baruch Brent will be interviewed by an online magazine. He will compare the circumstances of 1938 to the 21st century migrant crisis. Refugees of this new age, Leslie says, would probably give everything they could to pay back their new home countries for their generosity. He will talk about the nightmares he still has and about the guilt that just won't fade, however "irrational" it is. Leslie Baruch Brent's research will help save the lives of countless transplantation patients. And Great Britain saved him.[2]

* * * * *

The New Yorker keeps rejecting Ilse's short stories. They ask her to send other work, then they reject yet again. They print Bishop's fiction, even though Bishop says she has no idea how fiction even works. Bishop's short story "In the Village" appears in *The New Yorker*. It portrays a young girl and her institutionalized mother. Bishop tells Ilse that she just wrote down what she had experienced as a child, that there's really nothing more to it.[3]

Future scholars of literature will stress how much Elizabeth Bishop differed from other writers of her generation. While her peers wrote "confessional poetry" about their fathers, marriages, and nervous breakdowns, Bishop, critics say, refused to put her private life on display.[4] And yet some private material does appear in Bishop's oeuvre. And, certainly, there's at least one writer in this period who's even more hesitant to turn personal matters into literature.

✳ ✳ ✳ ✳ ✳

They've bought a prefab with a window. Kit's studio. It sits a few steps away from their house. Good light from the north and big enough even for very large paintings. In the mornings Kit steps out to produce art. Ilse sits down at the typewriter. The house is hers, for the time being.

In July 1954 Ilse meets with solicitor Lehmann. He asks questions about her father, her mother, her sister. Ilse doesn't have many answers, and Lehmann seems a bit irritated. He also wonders why she says that doesn't speak German. She sends him a letter a few days later and apologizes for being so "unhelpful." She says she knows he needs to talk about these things with her and that she really should help him to help her.

In the following year she keeps a diary: the "Amateur Gardening Diary and Horticultural Directory 1955." There's not much space for the daily entries as it is, and her handwriting's pretty large. On January 15 she notes: "Letter from Tony + from Tante Matilde." "Tante" is one German word she does use. Or is it French? On April 29 she writes: "Kohlrabi + flowers doing well." Apart from that it is a very English diary. She notes that there was rain, more rain, and then a sunny day. She records who came for tea, who spent the night, who they went to the movies with, to the pub. The dog had to be taken to the vet, and Kit cut down a crab tree, and Faber & Faber, an immensely renowned English publisher, is thinking about publishing Kathrine Talbot's *The Innermost Cage*. Her agent Elaine has let her know. This would mean that her second novel would appear on both sides of the Atlantic Ocean.

From the slush pile at Faber & Faber someone pulled out *Strangers from Within*. The novel will become one the most widely read books of its time. First, though, they're going to have to get the author to agree to a new title. Maybe this one: *Lord of the Flies*?

The "Book Committee" makes all the decisions at Faber & Faber. It consists entirely of men. There's a woman secretary who takes notes. Another woman prepares lunch. A few minutes before one o'clock, the tray with the drinks appears in the conference room. That's about the time when committee member T.S. Eliot shows up. He has just married a Faber & Faber secretary. Most days Eliot has a dry Martini.

Following drinks, there's lunch. Before the meal begins, the secretary must leave the room. That's how the rules are. After drinks and lunch, the men of the Book Committee and the secretary gather around an octagonal table to make decisions. There's this play called *Waiting for Godot*, for example. It's successful, no doubt about that. The Book Committee resolves to ask Samuel Beckett whether he would like to write a book with his personal memories. Something autobiographical, how about that? Beckett won't be interested. He will answer in French that he has fewer personal recollections than a six-month-old baby.[5]

The Book Committee also discusses Kathrine Talbot's work. There are consequences. "Feel too nervous to live!!!," Ilse Barker notes in the "Amateur Gardening Diary." On February 4, 1955, a letter arrives from London. Now she notes: "Excitement beyond belief! Dear God!" Faber & Faber hasn't just agreed to release *The Innermost Cage*. They also want to publish her next novel. On February 14, she notes: "All this success is bad for me." It's very cold and dark, she writes. She's worried about Kit, who isn't having enough success.

* * * * *

1955 brings an icy spring. Kit and Ilse have already used up all their firewood. Now they're wandering through the forest, picking up branches and twigs. Then it gets warmer, then it rains and rains.

They go to London. Kit's mother is dying. Kit sits down next to her bed. "Big Mumma" can't speak anymore. She has her purse next to her on the bed. She opens it. She takes coins from the purse, small ones, mid-sized ones, bigger ones, and, finally, a banknote. She pushes the money in Kit's direction and smiles at him, like she did back then, right after the war, just as the pubs were about to open.

Ilse's doing what Lehmann asked her to do. She's compiling a list of the household goods in Gaustraße 11 in Bingen, back in the good times. It's a difficult task. There were three pictures in the dining room. Oil paintings, possibly of some value. From the music room's ceiling hung a chandelier. Perhaps it was French. An Electrolux vacuum cleaner stood in the kitchen. A parasol on the balcony. The list grows longer.

Then she writes her life story. German authorities need this to process her application for reparation payments. She explains that antisemitic persecution was more "successful" in her small town than in the big cities. Everyone knew each other, so it wasn't long before Jewish citizens could no longer walk the streets. She explains the plans that her parents had made for her university education. She writes about her new, antisemitic teachers after 1933, her breakdown in 1935, and about Dr. Mehler's visit. She briefly explains how her mother's, father's and sister's lives ended. Then she sends off the document.

Lehmann answers that he needs more. The complete application requires three separate life histories, one each for the mother, father, and sister. Lehmann asks whether she might be able to write these in German. Then the documents wouldn't have to be translated. Ilse writes two typed pages per parent and a half page about Bertha. She mentions how, in April 1933, strands in her mother's hair suddenly turned white, right after the first boycott of Jewish businesses. She writes that her father was fifty-seven at the time, not an adaptable man, and nonetheless convinced that Nazi rule wouldn't last long. Her sister, Ilse states, had the mentality of a small child. From her home in Rhens on the Rhine, the Nazis took her to a Jewish institution in Bendorf-Sayn. From there she was deported.[6] Ilse notes an estimate of the date of her death: April 30,1942. Along with these accounts – all of them written in English – she sends Lehmann a letter. She tells him how strange it seems that her family's suffering was "such a common thing" and how probable it is, therefore, that readers of these stories won't feel any pain or compassion.

* * * * *

From time to time, the Olsons buy one of Kit's paintings and then some money comes in. That doesn't happen too often, though. Some of Kit's work is exhibited in London. There are good reviews, but no buyers. And Ilse isn't making much money either. Neither *Fire in the Sun* nor *The Innermost Cage* turn into commercial successes, not on either side of the Atlantic Ocean.

A friend of the Barkers has a large apple orchard. He hires them to help with the harvest. Per hour, male pickers make one shilling and eleven pence, female pickers one shilling and eight pence.

Then colleges in Oxford buy some of Kit Barker's pieces and the Federal Republic of Germany transfers the first reparation payments to their bank account, so they go off to Florence, Rome, Paestum, and Venice. They live with Italian families. Hotels are too expensive. Lunch consists of hard-boiled eggs eaten on a park bench. They stay in Italy until they are unquestionably out of money, again.

Kit has lost some of his shyness. In Italy he was able to pull out a sketch pad in a crowded place and not feel embarrassed. Strangers watched him draw and he didn't mind. Once they're back in England, American art collectors will show up. They'd like to see the Italian pictures.

* * * * *

Alongside the "Amateur Gardening Diary," Ilse keeps another notebook. Like Henry James, she collects the names of potential protagonists. She jots down last names like Millbourne, Cowley, Ferney, Misselbrook, Blessley and women's first names like Solange, Felicity, Miriam, Sally, Nan. She writes down ideas for a novel. She often thinks about an American who moves to England. Bob. "I shall have to *become* Bob," she notes. But how? It's difficult. Bob, she notes, "is only a fraction of myself + he is a man." And then she does conclude: "I *can* be Bob, I know it."

She sketches ideas for short stories. Like this one: A woman is artistically inclined, her husband isn't, but she realizes that he's intellectually superior to her nonetheless, and that depresses her. Her agent Elaine has another idea: What about a woman who falls in love with a painter and then sees his pictures and doesn't like them? Implausible, Ilse says. Love would change this woman's ideas about art.

She writes stories about artists, about marriage, about English middle-class realities. It appears as though she really thinks the biographies she sent to Lehmann were uninteresting, too much of a "common thing," and so she doesn't explore what's going on in a woman in an idyllic, antisemitic small town when she suddenly finds white strands in her hair. Nor does she deal with that woman's twelve-year old daughter and what these white strands might have meant to her. She explores Bob. He's supposed to take Nan to the country, but another woman comes along instead. That sounds like an idea. She enters in the notebook: "I don't think I really *feel* Bob's dilemma." But she keeps working on his story. There will come a time when autofiction will be the most glittering new trend in the literary world: fiction that reads like the author's life story, only ever so slightly changed.[7] Kathrine Talbot is working in a different era.

✳ ✳ ✳ ✳ ✳

A man named Victor Waddington opens a gallery in London. Ilse and Kit drive into the city. Ilse waits in the car. Kit disappears, five paintings under his arms. When he comes back, she sees only two paintings and a big smile on his face. They drive away from London and up Bexley Hill. They get out of the car. The neighbors beckon them over. They have a phone, the Barkers don't. Waddington's been calling. The three paintings have been sold. Would Kit perhaps have a few more?

✳ ✳ ✳ ✳ ✳

Ilse starts a new career as a translator from the German. There's a manuscript on her desk called *Noch leuchten die Bilder*, a work by the German art expert Hans H. Pars. "The pictures still shine," the original title says. The volume tells the stories of masterpieces: their "fates and adventures." How someone took a saw to cut the head of Saint Hieronymus out of a Leonardo painting. How Napoleon stole one of Titian's altarpieces. How the damp ceiling of the Sistine Chapel frustrated Michelangelo so much that he almost quit the job.[8]

Ilse finds it hard to read German again. The sentences are so long. So complicated. And the book comes to more than 400 pages. Like Michelangelo, she bemoans her fate. And then she barrels through.

She hands in the manuscript as Kathrine Talbot, not as Ilse Barker. It seems appropriate: "Hans H. Pars," after all, is also a pseudonym. Behind this one "Hans" are two actual men, and they both happen to be called Hans. One of them, Hans Schwarz van Berk, was a very early member of the Nazi Party, a Ministry for Propaganda official, and an SS man. The other, Hans Diebow, published an exultant Hitler biography as early as 1931 and a host of antisemitic diatribes after 1933 (*The Eternal Jew* is the most widely known). Given the new political framework, the two men called Hans have decided to reinvent themselves. They have merged into one connoisseur of art.[9]

* * * * *

On August 4, 1955, Ilse stops keeping the "Amateur Gardening Diary." Why she quits is unclear. She recorded numerous things the previous week. How she and Kit were a bit miffed because their friend Wally had asked them to send him the underwear he left behind during his last visit, which they did – and then Wally never thanked them. Kit was unhappy with a certain G. who didn't buy him a drink at the pub. G. may well stand for George. Kit and Ilse went to watch cricket. Ilse loves cricket. On another day, wonderfully sunny, they walked into the pub at twelve noon, stayed until four, went home, ate something and then lay on the grass. B. and A. were lying there with them. They are "so nice." A "lovely weekend," Ilse concluded. "Brenda drops in," she noted on Tuesday. Her final entry: They saw Hitchcock's *Rear Window* in Midhurst.

* * * * *

Ilse and Kit could be such great parents. That's Elizabeth Bishop's view of things from Brazil. They are so quiet, loving, and wise, Bishop says.

Lota and Bishop now have a pistachio green VW camper. Bishop has seen the new Queen in newsreels. When Elizabeth II. waves to her subjects, Bishop writes, her hand moves as if she were screwing in a lightbulb. Bishop's jealous of the parties Ilse and Kit are throwing, and jealous of the English pubs. She asks if Ilse has heard of the German poet Andreas Gryphius. She writes about the Brazilian national soccer team: about their strengths (magicians with the ball) and weaknesses (not good at teamwork). She writes that she, Bishop, has won the Pulitzer and that for three weeks reporters, radio people, and TV people have been dragging mud into the house, and that she, Bishop, appeared in the same newsreel as Grace Kelly. Crime in Brazil is on the rise and from time to time she borrows Lota's rifle for shooting practice. Bishop writes that she'd never thought Ilse and Kit might be planning to have a baby, as Ilse had mentioned in her last letter.

She'd always thought that the Barkers were too poor or maybe didn't want children because that would get in the way of the "artistic life." Or that maybe they were barren. Should that not be the case, Bishop recommends a book by developmental psychologist Arnold Gesell, *The Child from Birth to 5*, or, for long-term preparatory research, the same author's *The Child from 5 to 10*.

✷ ✷ ✷ ✷ ✷

Nine months. That is the length of time this young American spends in London. On business. Kathrine Talbot has called him Bob. A friend has introduced him to a London family, the Blessleys, an unconventional, chaotic lot. Bob often comes to visit – and he mainly comes for Nan, their strangely adorable daughter. Bob must live with the fact that in London his short American haircut is seen as an embarrassing attempt to overemphasize his masculinity. He also learns that in England a man should never try to understand a woman. That could be seen as unmanly. Bob, however, would be more than happy to at least partly understand this woman called Nan.

Kathrine Talbot designs her novel as a psychological study of her protagonists. Whatever's going on in Ilse Barker doesn't play a role for this project. She portrays Bob and Nan and Nan's brother and Nan's mother and a wide variety of emotional and communicative issues in their relationships. Then she analyses these complications once more, from a distance, by creating a second narrative level that presents Bob's life after his return to New York, and his elaborate accounts of his London experiences, to a first-person narrator thoroughly unfamiliar with Nan, Nan's mother, or any Blessley in the whole wide world. Like Henry James in his day, Kathrine Talbot unfolds the story of an innocent American confused by dubious Old World figures. As in James, there's little impulsive action. She writes about very thoughtful people with time on their hands and for thoughtful readers willing to take the time.[10]

Then Bob and a female companion are lying in a meadow far from London, in a secluded spot, and they've finished their picnic and she gives him this very specific look from beneath her eyelashes and then both of them don't think about much at all. In a truly un-Jamesian fashion they take action. Because neither of them has considered contraception and because this woman clearly isn't Nan – though Bob has never made a secret out of his adoration for Nan and only Nan – events unfold abruptly, as they rarely do in Kathrine Talbot's prose.

* * * * *

Bishop sends a parcel. It contains, among other things, Brazilian coffee, guava jam, and two kinds of salsa: "fearfully HOT so watch out." Again and again, Ilse sends her stories to Brazil. Bishop reads them. Between the lines of the letters she sends to Sussex there's a certain lack of enthusiasm. Bishop advises Ilse to get to the point more quickly. If she ever wants to sell a story to the *New Yorker*, Bishop says, her fiction needs to be much more specific. When Ilse tells her that she wants to call her new novel *Sabine*, Bishop warns that would sound too pretty. When the novel, now titled *Return,* has arrived in Brazil, not a single Sabine among the protagonists, Bishop praises Ilse's work. She doesn't use the most glowing terms, though.

In one of her letters, the Pulitzer Prize winner really gets going. She slanders the novelist Elizabeth Bowen. Bishop knows that her friend Ilse likes Bowen's work very much. But that doesn't stop her. And while she's at it, she attacks half a dozen other women writers too, who, as Bishop sees it, have the same problem, which is the typical women writers' way of seeing the world as too pretty, too "nice." How these women always brag, Bishop writes. There's always the beautifully polished silver and the tasteful dresses and the fabulous husbands. In Kathrine Talbot's new novel, too, no protagonist has ever experienced life outside of elegant metropolitan affluence, so Bishop must be aware that she's also attacking Ilse's work. She may not care. Should women writers want to achieve any kind of goal, Bishop notes, this whole "how nice to be nice" business is going to have to stop.

* * * * *

And then Ilse Barker must have opened up to Elizabeth Bishop about the fate of her family in the Nazi camps. In the autumn of 1958, she finally tells her. When she replies, Bishop writes to her, just to her, not to "Ilse and Kit" and not to the "Barkers," as she usually does. She writes that she gave Ilse's letter to Lota to read. That they stayed up all night talking about it. That they had tried to understand the world and the times they lived in. "I am very touched that you will tell me these things," Bishop writes in her letter, "and of course I had wondered and thought all these years and sensed something of the whole tragedy." Only now had she realized what a miracle it was that Ilse escaped and survived. "There is really nothing one can say, is there."

Bishop wants to do something for her. And for Kit. She invites them to Brazil. They should stay for a year, she writes. They could get some sun and swim. Lead a simpler life. With a little bit of money, she says, Ilse could afford to have a maid in Brazil and dedicate all her time to her writing. She says that after very dark times, she, Bishop, had found true happiness in Brazil.

Elizabeth Bishop knows almost no German. To conclude this letter to Ilse, though, she types a German-language poem. It consists of eight lines. Composed during the horrors of the Thirty-Years War, it presents an elegy to a child that died just a few weeks after her birth. Sitting at her typewriter in Brazil, Elizabeth Bishop copies Andreas Gryphius' 17th century "Epitaph of Marianne Gryphius, Daughter of His Brother Paul:"

> Geboren in der Flucht, umringt mit Schwert und Brand,
> Schier in dem Rauch erstickt, der Mutter herbes Pfand,
> Des Vatern höchste Furcht, die an das Licht gedrungen,
> Als die ergrimmte Glut mein Vaterland verschlungen:
> Ich habe diese Welt beschaut und bald gesegnet,
> Weil mir auf Einen Tag all' Angst der Welt begegnet;
> Wo ihr die Tage zählt, so bin ich jung verschwunden,
> Sehr alt, wofern ihr schätzt, was ich für Angst empfunden.

Maybe, though, Bishop assumes in her letter, Ilse knows this elegy to a dead little girl by heart.

9

Thomas

Never talk about babies. That was the unwritten law among the bohemian women in postwar Cornwall. Not even the slightest joke was allowed. They were all superstitious. If you mentioned anything remotely related to reproduction, you got pregnant immediately, no question about it. And in New York City, Ilse had a slight falling out with her Catholic colleagues in "Media Typing," because, making small talk in that windowless office one day, she'd said something vaguely critical about motherhood. Always better to leave that topic well alone. Even in her fiction women don't have babies. In *Return*, when a certain someone's expecting, after a picnic in the country, her main protagonist escapes in a flash, across the Atlantic Ocean, and the pregnant woman disappears from the pages of her book.

Much later, one of Ilse Barker's friends will tell an interviewer that Ilse didn't want children because she had never gotten over losing her parents. "She didn't want to lose anything of her own blood again." That's how this witness will put it. In a letter to Bishop, however, Ilse mentions that medical complications got in the way.

* * * * *

Ilse and Kit won't move to Brazil. *Return* comes out in 1959. The London *Times* praises how lovingly the story is told and how elegantly the author interweaves background and character studies. The *Times Literary Supplement* finds Bob's confusion touching. The two temporal levels, though, à la Joseph Conrad, seem a bit complicated to the *TLS. Books and Bookmen* complains about a certain "artificiality" in Kathrine Talbot, but it does declare *Return* "a most gripping novel." *The Irish Times* says that this was probably a book more liked by women than by men. Then they add a "but." A "but" seems necessary. And after that "but," *The Irish Times* explains that so much contemporary literature lacked a sense of style and that therefore Talbot's elegant *Return* should not be underestimated. The

Belfast News calls her technique "masterful." And the *Manchester Guardian*, soon just the *Guardian*, loves how the novel made British readers feel "European, complex, and a little bit dangerous." The *Guardian*'s critic wants to read more by Kathrine Talbot. He calls her a "natural novelist."

* * * * *

Holding a divining rod in his hand, a friend of the Barkers meets them on Bexley Hill. Together they climb further up the hill. The rod starts moving and they start digging. They find a spring. Now they can build water tanks in the area above the cottage. The water flows into the tanks and from the tanks into the water pipes that now lead to their house. They install an indoor toilet and then electricity and a telephone. The government will pass a law regulating the minimum height of ceilings and as a result they will receive public funding and be able to lower the floor. Once that's done, they'll stand in their house and hold their heads up high.

And the natural novelist who hasn't had a baby by the age of forty and is surely never going to have babies has a baby when she's forty-one years old. Thomas Crispin Barker. His birthday, 26-11-62, is a palindrome. That makes his mother happy. On Tom's birth certificate it says "Artist-Painter" under "Father's Profession." The form has no column for "Mother's Profession."

Tom is an upbeat, balanced child who sleeps a lot. You can take him down the hill in a pram, to The Horseshoe, the closest pub; there you can carry the child upstairs to a bedroom above the pub and put him in landlady Marjorie Bathgate's bed. You can have a few beers at the pub and, after closing time, lift the child from Marjorie's bed, place him back in the pram and push pram and baby back up the hill. Tom grows to be a boy who loves strolling through the woods with his friends, a boy who likes singing, an optimistic boy. Relatively early in his life, Ilse will tell him about the fate of his grandparents and his aunt. After that she will remain almost completely silent on these matters. In contrast to his father, Tom will study at an art school. At some point Ilse is going to tell Tom and his friends that to remain creative they should never in their lives take on a regular full-time job. Tom will heed that advice.

Kit and Ilse are pretty unconventional – and then again, Ilse's responsible for the household and for Tom. Kit's art is more important than Ilse's writing. Now that his career has finally taken off, he'll have to keep working hard. The wonderful reviews for *Return* don't change the roles in their marriage.

They replace the prefab with a real studio. In the morning Kit leaves the house, sits down, reads the paper or a crime novel, and at some point, the exact time of which cannot be foreseen, he gets up, steps over to the easel, and begins. That's the magic moment: the first time the brush touches the whiteness of the canvas.

The author named Kathrine Talbot doesn't have a room of her own, only a table with a typewriter on it. Later Tom will recall how on sunny days his mother often sat in front of the house, reading. But she can't have possibly found a lot of time for this. She's not only Tom's mother; she's also the adviser and motivational coach for artist Kit Barker. At some point each day she must make Kit put away the novel or the paper and finally start painting. If she didn't tell him, he never would.

* * * * *

In 1964 Bishop comes for a visit. They haven't seen each other in fourteen years. Bishop inspects the tanks and the pipes and the house. She looks around in the kitchen. Then she goes away, to London, comes back to Bexley Hill, and opens a bag. She has bought the utensils Ilse seems to be lacking. A vegetable steamer. A knife to cut tomatoes with. Then she takes the ship back to Brazil.

Ilse doesn't enjoy cooking. But she must cook, and when she's cooking, she listens to the Archers. There's a new episode every day, five days a week. Jennifer isn't married and yet – how is that even possible? – she gives birth to a child. She doesn't want to tell anyone whose baby it is, but the child does resemble the cowhand on Brookfield Farm.[1] The Barkers always eat at twenty minutes past seven because Ilse listens to the Archers until seven fifteen.

Their house frequently fills up with guests. They have fun dinners with artists, writers, art critics, even the Olsons, who come flying in sometimes. It goes without saying that Kit, who has lost much of his shyness and probably doesn't feel eclipsed by big brother George anymore, sits there all evening entertaining their guests with his witty stories, his profound knowledge of the Middle Ages, and the Irish folk songs he sings. And if a child appears in front of him, he'll place his hands on either side of the little one's face and kiss its cheeks, once on the right and once on the left, such a truly loveable man and a fascinating artist – and it also goes without saying that before, during, and after these wonderful evenings, Ilse's taking care of the shopping, cooking, doing the dishes, and cleaning up.

Kit's domestic chores consist of drying the dishes and going to the woods to forage for mushrooms, when they're in season. It's hard for Ilse to find time to write. But she does. Somehow, the writer known as Kathrine Talbot manages to finish another novel. It's sent off to Faber & Faber and she hopes for the best.

⁕ ⁕ ⁕ ⁕ ⁕

Her agent Elaine is doing whatever she can for Ilse. But she has also found the manuscript for a detective novel that someone pushed under her office door. P.D. James. Nobody knows who P.D. James is. Then again, Faber & Faber do need a new mystery author. The old one just died. They find out that this Mr. James is actually a Mrs. White, a Londoner in her forties working for the North West Metropolitan Hospital Board. They call Mrs. White and she says she also has ideas for a few other books. Around a dozen crime novels later, bestselling author Phyllis Dorothy White will be made a baroness by Her Majesty the Queen.[2]

Kathrine Talbot's *Return* hasn't sold too well. Maybe that's why the Book Committee takes a while to think about her new novel. At the press, they're also busy turning the many "fucking"s in a manuscript by former primary school teacher John McGahern into "f—"s and then, on McGahern's insistence, turn the "f—"s back into "fucking"s. Faber & Faber publishes *The Bell Jar*, Sylvia Plath's novel. It is released three years after the author's suicide, the most major literary event anyone could have conceived. The press receives a nasty letter from Philip Larkin, author of some of the most beautiful love poetry in the English language – or any language, for that matter. Larkin doesn't want to read "spy rubbish, science fiction rubbish, Negro-homosexual rubbish, or dope-taking nervous-breakdown rubbish" in books published by Faber & Faber.[3] They write a nuanced reply to Larkin. They also send a note to Kathrine Talbot in Sussex; unfortunately, they won't be able to publish her latest novel.

She won't find another publisher either. Is it because Faber & Faber's judgement counts for so much? Or is this novel just not very good? It's impossible to find out. She won't hold on to the manuscript. Did she not have enough time for writing? Would she have needed a room of her own? Or has she fallen behind the times? It is impossible that she feels how Larkin feels. Never would she write a letter like that. And then, her gentle realism may seem a bit conservative now.

* * * * *

For Tom's sixth birthday, in 1968, Ilse makes a cake in the form of a locomotive. Given her limited baking skills, she's very proud of this achievement. Elizabeth Bishop writes from San Francisco about one of her dinner parties where marijuana brownies were served. Ilse is surprised. She had always thought, she writes to Bishop, that the substance could only be smoked. She forgives Elizabeth for forgetting Tom's birthday. And she praises him in her letter. Such a cheerful boy. Always happy, always content. The third best singer in the entire school. Like father, like son.

* * * * *

Elaine, now the top agent of top author P.D. James, doesn't always personally attend to Ilse anymore, and Elaine's assistant Ilsa frustrates Kathrine Talbot. Ilse keeps sending Ilsa new short stories, and every time Ilsa tells Ilse that this story will be super easy to sell and then she doesn't manage to sell it after all. Ilse is convinced, she writes to Bishop, that she'll only have to sell one story, just one, to any magazine at all, and then things would take off right away. She knows these are good stories, but it just feels so ridiculous to always be rejected. Gingerly, Bishop advises that in Ilse's stories the introductory part sometimes seems a bit long and the dramatic part kicks in a bit late and might she perhaps want to turn that around?

* * * * *

Then they're lying on the beach and they're fighting. It's his infidelity, again, and it's one of those fights that could end a relationship. They're in Heyst, Belgium. And as they fight, they're watching something in the surf, something that's jumping around in the waves, something big and yellow. They feel that whatever it is they're seeing doesn't really belong on a North

Sea beach. Is it a lion? It looks like it. Really? It's getting closer. And that's making them far more tense than their fight.

She finds an ending for this story and she sends it to Elaine and Elaine sends it to the *Paris Review* and then, who would have thought, George Plimpton gets in touch, star author, friend of the Kennedys, international mover and shaker. He doesn't turn directly to Ilse, of course. He calls Roberta Pryor at International Famous Agency, New York, and Roberta gets in touch with Elaine in London. Roberta tells Elaine and Elaine tells Ilse that Plimpton would like to know who this Kathrine Talbot is: "what she's done, what she's doing now and what she will be doing." And whether this Kathrine Talbot would object to making a few cuts in her story.

Ilse has been writing short stories for twenty-five years. This is the first one that's going to be published. She asks Elaine whether that counts as some sort of record. She feels that the story is short enough as it is. But of course she agrees to make cuts.

"The Lion of Heyst" appears in 1971. Kathrine Talbot, fifty years old, now a *Paris Review* author, enjoys international recognition. Not much follows, however. *Mademoiselle* in New York rejects one of her stories. They express an interest in seeing some of her other work and that's the end of that. Her agent tells her that the editors of women's magazines tend to be inexplicable figures. Sometimes it seems they want to offer their readers something different to the typical romantic fare, and then, when push comes to shove, they go for the schmaltziest love stories. Ilse's working on a new novel. What happens to the project is unclear. A New York publisher seems interested, then communication peters out. She's going to write two ghost stories, one for the *Midnight Ghost Book*, another for the *After Midnight Ghost Book*. One of these stories is set in Bingen. The story revolves around spooky cellars filled with casks of wine. It does not explore the horrors of German antisemitism. Kathrine Talbot still believes literature shouldn't relate to facts, only to whatever the subconscious has turned reality into. That's what makes fiction, she says. Everything else is just journalism.

✶ ✶ ✶ ✶ ✶

Waddington in London sever their ties with Kit. These days there's not much need for what he's painting: this combination of abstraction and landscape, that depth, these horizons. They now want color field painting by completely abstract Americans. And so the gallery schedules one last meeting with Kit. He drives their small car to London, the car that he always repairs himself, and then he comes back on this rainy day and the car's filled with all the paintings they asked him to please take along with him.

* * * * *

The Barkers are accustomed to living modest lives. Now they're going to need a bit more modesty. Nonetheless, the three of them go on a holiday in France. Tom is eleven or twelve. His adult memories of the trip will be vague. It must have been around Easter. He recalls snow in the Alsace. And the strange roofs of Colmar. He also remembers how they crossed the border to Germany. How they went to Bingen. How his mother returned to her hometown for the first time in forty years. Tom saw the Rhine, he'll later say, and train tracks and trains.

It's all a bit fuzzy, but there's one thing Tom remembers very well. They had just arrived in Bingen, Ilse, Kit, and Tom. They'd gotten out of the car and begun to stroll through the streets and then suddenly turned around, very abruptly, really, and headed back to the car. They got in. They drove off. The end of the visit. Once Bingen was behind them, Tom's parents explained to him that his mother hadn't wanted to stay a moment longer.

* * * * *

Her son loves playing polo. Maybe he loves it a bit too much. When he can't play polo, he sits at home on a wooden horse and practices hitting balls into a net with his stick. After one polo match, he meets the eloquent Camilla. She marries someone else, however. After another polo match, he will have the first of several long conversations with an almost childlike young woman named Diana, who at this point in time seems very enthusiastic about spending time with him.

With his stick in hand, his horse between his thighs, her son rides up and down the field of Cowdray Park Polo Club in Midhurst, Sussex. Sometimes she watches his matches. She is his mother, after all. In Midhurst people know what the Queen looks like. They haven't just seen her on TV.[4]

Ilse Barker's son plays soccer, not polo. She goes to the butchers in Midhurst to pick up something for supper. She opens the door to the shop. The shop assistants look at her. They seem incredulous. And subservient. And speechless. But they probably soon realize that Ilse Barker's not the Queen.

* * * * *

As Kathrine Talbot she translates a novel called *Der Mädchenkrieg*. The book's set in Prague, during World War Two. It says nothing at all about the mass murder of Czech Jews by the Germans, and it's a great success in Germany. She translates a thriller about a gangster abducting the daughter of a German tank manufacturer. She translates a retelling of Wagner's operas and a coffee-table book by Leni Riefenstahl. The former Nazi propagandist portrays the Maasai, their spears and shields, the supple way they move their bodies. "A proud people," Riefenstahl calls them. Kathrine Talbot translates.[5]

* * * * *

Sometimes weeks go by without any sign that the art world remembers Kit. No calls. No letters. Kit has a prescription for new glasses, and he puts them on and paints a painting of a waterfall and hangs it on the wall of the living room, and Ilse loves that painting, even though it's maybe a bit large for that particular wall. Then again: maybe it's the living room that's too small.

After all these quiet weeks, a young couple comes up the hill. The husband bought one of Kit's paintings two years ago. On this summer afternoon he buys another one and these two pictures, the new and the old one, the couple says, will hang next to each other in their new Paris apartment. The young man says that the walls in their French salon will have a very original look. "DARK BLUE VELVET," Ilse writes to Bishop. "Unbelievable."

And then, at long last, she takes the material she knows, stuff from her life, the German-Jewish stories she's familiar with, and writes about the refugees from Bingen and their postwar lives. She makes these people her protagonists and tells of their narrow escapes and their courageous struggles. She has finally managed to cross the distance between Ilse Gross from Bingen and Kathrine Talbot, British writer. She sends the story to agent Elaine and waits for an answer.

* * * * *

With her friend Esther, Ilse laughs a lot. As a sixteen-year-old girl, Esther appeared night after night at "Chez Eve" in Paris. In the nude. Esther's mother had arranged the job for her daughter. Maybe not a choice every mother would make. On stage, Esther wore nothing but a tambourine around her hips. It was supposed to look as if she had accidentally stepped into the instrument. In her hand she held an umbrella. Then she danced to "Lady Be Good."

After her initial shame had subsided, there was something enjoyable about these performances. What Esther particularly liked, however, was getting dressed after her shift was over and going to some all-night restaurant for steak frites and rum and coke. That was the perfect life, Esther felt, until another dancer informed the police and Esther had to return to her mother in London. It turned out she was still a little young to be dancing in the nude.[6]

When Esther comes to Bexley Hill she brings her husband, John, one of Kit and George's nephews. Then the women go off for a walk in the country and the men stay in the house. Esther and John sometimes have George over, which Ilse and Kit rarely do these days, and then John and George get drunk together. That doesn't always end well. On one occasion George ran into the garden, furious and wasted, and he returned to the house with an axe in his hand. Esther hid behind the sofa and eventually the genius poet put the axe away.

Like Ilse, Esther fled Germany as a child. She escaped with her mother and her sister. Her father remained in Cologne and was later killed in Auschwitz. On one of their walks Esther suggests they speak German. Hers is so rusty. They could practice. Ilse declines.

* * * * *

Ilse hears that Elizabeth Bishop left Lota Macedo Soares and Brazil. Later, visiting Bishop in New York, Lota takes an overdose of valium and dies.

"No coffee can wake you no coffee can wake you no coffee:" lines written by Bishop, to Lota, after her death.[7]

In 1979 Bishop once again visits the Barkers, now with Alice, her new partner. Ilse sees the two off, to the bus going to Heathrow. She waves after the bus. A few months later, Bishop dies. Ilse keeps cutting tomatoes with the knife that Bishop bought for her. She calls it "Elizabeth's tomato knife."

* * * * *

Then agent Elaine is done reading the short story about the refugees from Bingen, their German pasts, and their new lives. And she tells Ilse what she thinks. The passage about the Final Solution, for example, and the one about the gas chambers? Elaine says there's really no need to mention all of that. Won't readers already be familiar with these things? Ilse makes cuts where cuts need to be made and sends the story back to Elaine. After that, no further traces of the piece can be found. There are many short stories in Kathrine Talbot's papers. This one she doesn't keep.

10

The Door

In the 1980s Kathrine Talbot writes a poem about a car wash. The jungle of giant brushes. The monsoon engulfing the car. For forty years she has heeded the advice received on the Isle of Man: better not to write poetry in English. Having Bishop as a friend made it impossible to try, in any case. But Bishop's death has cleared the way. Kathrine Talbot writes poetry now. The form she chooses isn't overly strict, and she writes about her everyday experiences. She writes about art, about books, and, if necessary, about a car wash. We should kiss stormily, the poetic voice says amid the jungle of brushes. We should kiss before the washing cycle ends.

* * * * *

The polo-crazy prince goes to Liverpool. It is May 1988. Like Ilse in 1940, they take him to the warehouses by the docks. Nobody throws stones at him. He's standing behind a lectern, utters a few well-chosen words, and then takes a small step to the side and pulls on a cord. A curtain opens and reveals the plaque which makes the reopening of "Albert Dock" official. Later, at Tate Liverpool, the gallery that has moved into the warehouses, the prince looks at contemporary art. Three men around him explain the pieces. The prince seems to be listening. He massages his left wrist with his right hand.

Ilse Barker won't let go of her antipathy toward Liverpool. But she understands the reasoning behind her internment. She calls it a panicked reaction on the part of the British government, and she will see no similarity whatsoever between her camp on the Isle of Man and any of the German camps on the Continent. She doesn't regard what happened to her in 1940 as an act of organized violence. To her it was "a muddle."

One time in June 1988, Kit wakes up in the middle of the night. His back aches. He feels sick to the stomach. He throws up again and again. In the morning he shows no sign of improvement, so Ilse calls the local health center. Dr. Guthrie's on call. He says that unfortunately for Ilse he'll have the afternoon off and suggests that Ilse call Dr. Davis.

Kit remains in bed. Ilse makes him some peppermint tea. He throws up again. And then she opens the front door, and there's Dr. Guthrie, who thought he'd stop by just to check. He checks. And then he asks Ilse if she'd like to walk him to his car.

✴ ✴ ✴ ✴ ✴

Now Kathrine Talbot translates German's children's books. She turns the volume *Ein gutes Schwein bleibt nicht allein* into *A Pig That Is Kind Won't Be Left Behind* and *Was für ein Tag* into *What a Day*.[1] She also translates from the French. First comes a novel about sexual violence (the *New York Times* finds her translation "merely workmanlike"). Then it's a collection of surrealist short stories (the *New York Times* calls her translation "elegant").[2] And she scouts books for a publisher. She reads and evaluates a nonfiction book about the Catholic Church and its relationship to sexuality ("Whatever next," she comments) and a novel about Charlotte Corday, killer of Jean Paul Marat, in his bathtub, guillotined in 1793.

✴ ✴ ✴ ✴ ✴

She's standing in front of Dr. Guthrie's car, and they talk, and she doesn't look at Dr. Guthrie. She looks at this one tire of his car. Guthrie is fairly certain that Kit's liver cancer has returned, three years after going into remission, and that it must have spread quickly. He says that Ilse should talk to Kit, because it could all happen in a very short time. Six months, perhaps. The one tire she keeps looking at will burn itself into her brain.

Six days later a test confirms Dr. Guthrie's suspicion. Kit and Ilse talk it over. Kit seems shocked, but he doesn't say much. They both have a glass of whisky.

She makes Kit things to eat, he throws up, she makes him something else, he develops a cough, she makes tea. She writes to friends and relatives that there's really not much hope. She also sends a few lines to George. She reads a story by A.S. Byatt about a woman unable to grieve because she has been through extreme grief before. "I fear this too," Ilse types in the diary she's started to keep. She reminds Kit to drink. She does the laundry. She helps Kit into the tub and back out.

When he's asleep she sits down at the typewriter and writes about his mother's death. About how quickly it went. The reservations she'd had, about "Big Mumma," because Kit's mother washed her feet in the same bowl in which she cleaned the potatoes and the dishes. How awful she, Ilse, had found the "Catholic thing" back then – how the Barkers had kept the picture of the pope in a cheese package on their wall, Pius XII looking out from beneath the transparent lid. "I suppose I was just hopelessly middle-class," Ilse writes.

Kit gets a bit better, then a bit worse. "Up and down we go," she writes. His face seems sunken. The end is near. "I can't live without him," she says to herself, out loud, every now and then. He keeps throwing up. He has these interminable hiccups. When Tom's visiting, he's twenty-five now, she tells him that his father is going to die very soon. She can only tell him because Tom's fixing the lawnmower at the same time. He's tinkering with the machine, and she tells him everything, and Thomas, she writes later, "was perfect, of course, calm and supportive." Every day now seems very long to her.

* * * * *

In St. Austell, Cornwall, just six miles from Mevagissey, a woman named Karen Gershon is writing an introduction to a book. Once her name was Käthe Löwenthal. That was in Bielefeld, Germany. In the 1960s she interviewed 233 people saved by the Kindertransport and turned these conversations into a collective biography. The book will get a new edition.

Karen Gershon herself was on the Kindertransport. Now she's a mother and a grandmother, a woman in her mix-sixties, and she writes how even now, half a century later, she's unable to develop proper relationships with people. She's still fighting the conviction that individuals aren't really important. Her parents were enslaved and killed, she says, "as if they did not matter." If that applied to her parents, wouldn't it also apply to everyone else, including herself, Karen Gershon? She can't let go of that idea.[3]

* * * * *

Ilse cut Kit's hair from 1947 onwards. The first time was in Mevagissey, when it was far too long on his collar.

She loved his voice. The Barkers always sang a lot, sometimes too much, but this particular Barker had a truly wonderful voice. Back in New York, shy Kit appeared on the radio once, singing Irish folk songs.

He liked painting sheep, not just fish. When she gives up the cottage on Bexley Hill and moves to Midhurst, a few miles away, one of his sheep paintings goes up on the wall of her new dining room. One sheep in the foreground, the other resting in the background. At first you think the sheep in front is more important for the painting than the other. And then you reconsider.

Kit. Albert Gordon Barker. A few years later she writes a poem about grief and about the return of happiness. About flowers that bloom again and cherries that ripen. About harvesting apples: the fruit on the shelves. And how some nights, alone in the double bed, pain stings the heart. Deeper than on the first day.

✶ ✶ ✶ ✶ ✶

An article appears in the American journal *Contemporary Literature*. The piece discusses her, Ilse Barker. Not Kathrine Talbot. Ilse. And Kit. And Bishop. A scholar named Victoria Harrison has examined the letters they exchanged. Harrison notes that Bishop had other, more famous pen friends than the Barkers. There was the great poet Robert Lowell, for one. Lowell, however, couldn't be bothered with everyday details, nor with Bishop's personal troubles. He kept having his own dramatic breakdowns and he expected Bishop's letters to respond to these because to him they seemed so much more important than any crisis she was experiencing. Bishop's letters to the even greater poet Marianne Moore were shaped by admiration and respect. It was taboo, though, to tell Moore anything about Bishop's love life and just as unthinkable to mention anything remotely political. No rules governed the Bishop-Barkers correspondence. In *Contemporary Literature*, Victoria Harrison concludes: "They loved her and she them, unconditionally and unproblematically." These letters, she says, were more explicit, more loving, and more intimate than all other exchanges.[4]

✶ ✶ ✶ ✶ ✶

In London Ilse runs into George. He's in a wheelchair now. She kneels to give him a hug. There was a time, in the pubs after the war, when George kicked her shin when he didn't like something she'd said. Years later, witnesses will emphasize that, in 1940s Cornwall, Ilse Pittock-Buss did not have intimate relations with George Barker.

In 1935 George gouged out Kit's eye. Then he wrote a poem about the event and about the guilt he felt. He wrote that his hand had destroyed "the palace" of his brother's face and that nothing could ever make up for that: no accomplishments, no riches, not any form of beauty – "the blue tulip, the forget-me-not, or the sky."[5]

In New York Ilse wrote a short story called "The Blue Tulip" and she used lines from George's poem as the story's epigraph. She always knew that there was George the poet and George the person. If she found something in his poems that wouldn't let go of her, she saw no reason to fight it.

* * * * *

Ilse Barker – not Kathrine Talbot – travels to Poughkeepsie, New York. She has been invited to the 1992 "Elizabeth Bishop Symposium" at Vassar College. Experts give talks about Bishop's syntax, about Bishop and Walcott, Bishop and Wordsworth, Bishop and Auden, and about religious, ethnographic, feminist, and economic aspects of Bishop's poetry. Ilse sits on a panel called "Questions of Biography." She grasps the opportunity to tell these Bishop scholars about her profound mistrust of biography and any sort of history writing in general. She speaks as a former inhabitant of Bingen on the Rhine. She explains how the Easter school holidays there were extended in 1933 so that the history books could be rewritten. Once the school doors had opened again, the German past looked completely different.

* * * * *

She's in her seventies now. She listens to classical music on the radio. BBC Radio 3. She listens to "Gardener's Question Time" on Radio 4. They explore the issue whether fallen leaves should be raked from the lawn or not. She thinks that's an excellent question.

When someone comes to visit, she politely turns off the radio. Biscuits for tea never stay in the package. She always arranges them on a plate. Once a week Peggy comes in, her cleaning lady. But Peggy doesn't clean much.

They talk. Peggy needs that. Her son has an animal pension in Canada. Her daughter died from a heroin overdose.

Nobody sits as upright as Ilse does. Her back doesn't touch the back of the chair. People describe her as "measured." Some use the word "regal." Like the Queen? Like a more slender, more attractive version of the Queen. That's how Sue, her daughter-in-law, sees it.

Once Ilse dreams of the queen and turns that dream into a poem. The corgis are barking at her feet. Prince Philip is on the phone. And the speaker gets lost in the palace, a mixture of grand hotel and maze. The carpets are very deep.

Sue and Ilse go for a walk and Sue tells Ilse about this book she's reading, Primo Levi's Auschwitz account. Ilse changes the subject.[6]

When she's speaking German, she has an English accent. She sounds like a Genevan when she's speaking French. English she speaks in the neutral "Received Pronunciation." Some say she speaks the "Queen's English," but that's not the case. A linguist notes that after all these years of her reign, the Queen is the only person speaking the "Queen's English."[7] When Ilse speaks, you can't make out what part of England she's from. She speaks as if she had a plum in her mouth.

✳ ✳ ✳ ✳ ✳

In the final years of the 20th century autobiographies and biographies are more popular than ever. All lives are waiting to be told. There are the lives of writers and artists, from a Freudian or from a feminist perspective. The lives of football players, successful cyclists, and unhappily married princesses. Relationship stories of fathers and sons, mothers and daughters. The lives of immigrants and refugees and the lives of their children. Lives with AIDS. Lives with depression. Lives in dysfunctional families. Lives with addictions or lives lived with people living with addictions. The life of a man who as a child survived the German death camps and who now, as an old Jewish man in Switzerland, presents autobiographical fragments. It turns out that these fragments are complete fictions and that he's not a Jew. It isn't the only autobiographical account released during this time that doesn't stick to the facts. To keep track of things, scholars develop categories for the numerous life story variants. They use the term "gastrography" for an autobiographical work in which cooking plays a central role. An "ecobiography" mostly takes place outdoors. The "nobody memoir" tells the life story of a person nobody's heard of before its publication. The dominant genre in Britain is the "misery memoir."[8]

* * * * *

Kathrine Talbot's distaste for autobiographical writing seems to fade away at around this time. She's probably working on a book about her life. But nobody hears about it. She keeps these things to herself.

Her poems she does share with others. And maybe writing poetry has made it possible for her to tell her true story in prose. Like Elizabeth Bishop before her, she understands poems as a nonfictional art form.[9]

One of her poems portrays the well-behaved poets of today, how they gently clear their throats before reading, and it contrasts them with the wild poets back then, who were so poor and so furious, who harangued everything and everyone, in the pub or in bed. One of her poems probably sketches the young woman she shared a mattress with on the Isle of Man. It speaks of the "transitory love" the speaker felt for this woman. It evokes her eyes, her amber hair, the warm days spent on the cliffs together.

And then there's a prose piece that demonstrates that Ilse Barker/Kathrine Talbot has finally, after decades, decided to write about her life. It describes fishermen in leopard-patterned swimwear and Cornwall farmers setting fires on the moors. She evokes how one of the farmer's sons jumped around with his torch until the flames lit up the sky, and she reflects how the painter Kit Barker found inspiration in this scene. Wasn't novelist Kathrine Talbot also drawn back to these flames, writing *Fire in the Sun*? She doesn't say.

A St. Ives gallery publishes her essay in 1993, as a booklet titled *Kit Barker Cornwall 1947-1948*. They print two hundred copies. Time and time again people are going to write to her after reading this memoir. It's so strange. She'll say that nothing she ever wrote was as successful as that little book about Kit.

* * * * *

The scholar Marianne Hirsch introduces a term called "postmemory." It refers to a form of memory that individuals haven't personally experienced.

It's fully mediated: by stories, pictures, other documents. Studying this concept Hirsch explores how the children of survivors remember the Holocaust. But surely the children and siblings of the non-survivors can also be filled with "postmemory." The approach doesn't imply that memory could just evaporate and trauma overcome. "Postmemory" can and will be obsessive and burdensome, like personal memory, but it's more indirect, more fragmentary.[10]

In 2001 Ilse Barker turns eighty. Three times a year – for Pessach, Rosh Hashanah, for her birthday – a lady from Bingen writes to her. She belongs to a committee called "Arbeitskreis Jüdisches Bingen" and sends out letters to emigrated Jews and their descendants. "Liebe Frau Goetz," Ilse begins the letters in which she sends thanks to the lady from Bingen for these messages. Then she continues in English.

Ilse can't read the *Diary of Anne Frank*. She holds the book in her hands. She reads a few pages. Then she stops. She just can't. She puts the book away.

* * * * *

When Allegra and Louis come to visit their grandmother – it happens three times a year, roughly, not much more often, as they live far away, in Wales – she opens the door and says "hello." Louis is still a child then, but later, as a young man in his mid-twenties, he will still hear that "hello" in his head. The way Grandma Ilse talks is the most English accent he's ever heard. The "o" in "hello" isn't just an "o." It's a diphthong: after the "ll" there's a soft "ə"-sound and only after this "ə" does she get to the "o."

If her grandchildren use slang, Ilse corrects them. She also doesn't approve of the fact that more and more people these days use "less" when they should say "fewer." When relatives come to visit from Israel, Ilse's British family members are very surprised to hear her speak German.

She never talks about herself, about her past. For her grandchildren she always stocks up on Canada Dry Ginger Ale. She never throws food away. All leftovers go into the fridge, wrapped, boxed, with little stickers on them signifying what's inside. She wears elegant, colorful clothes, very different from other pensioners, who are mostly beige. When her grandchildren are visiting, she takes them to the stationery shop in Midhurst. For little Louis, one thing's obvious: "this is where she gets her stuff."

* * * * *

Ilse writes letters to Tom. She calls him Thomas. From the late 1980s to 2006 she writes every few weeks. First, she uses a typewriter, then a computer connected to a very bad printer. Then she buys a better printer.

She writes to Tom: "How much I miss laughing." But she doesn't lead a lonely life. Her letters are filled with reports about lunch and dinner dates, movie nights, visits to neighbors and visits from neighbors, trips to London with friends. With Bronnie and Amy she strolls through the Tate Gallery. She notes how beautiful the Matisses are. They're on loan from the Museum of Modern Art, from the big Matisse hall there, the one, she writes, she always loved to sit in, back in the New York days. It seems she didn't always wait in the lobby for Kit.

She listens to Wynton Marsalis. She steps out into the garden, wanting to let the sun dry her hair. A cup of tea in hand, she sits down on what she thinks is her last remaining stable garden chair. The chair collapses. She writes to Tom about the catastrophe. It certainly wasn't easy to get up out of the ruins of that chair.

And then real tragedy strikes. Over the last few years, she's been writing a new novel and she got it finished and was satisfied with it and sent it to Elaine and then she didn't hear from her for a very long time. Her agent couldn't muster the courage to tell her what she thought. Then they had an honest conversation and Elaine advised her to stick to translating; it seemed to be going really well, she said.

That hits Ilse "pretty hard." The effect, she says: "demoralizing." She keeps writing, but she doesn't tell Tom much about it. On one occasion she sends him a story because he asked for it. On another, she sends a poem. The mayor of Bingen keeps sending letters to her. "He likes to keep in touch," she comments. In the new 573-page biography of George Barker, countless mistakes annoy her. Biographies are so useless, she writes. Think about Larkin: how much she loves Larkin's poems and how utterly uninterested she is in Larkin the person.

She teaches courses for people with reading and writing disabilities. She takes an "Italian for Beginners" course. She attends funerals. How strange it is when everyone's crying except for her. Simply because she can't. She can't bear to see someone take a shovel and throw earth into the open grave. On the trip back from one of these funerals, she misses a train and then finds herself on the platform with a horde of Liverpool supporters, Liverpool!, but then they turn out to be really fine human beings.

She writes that she hates the word "prestigious." She goes to see Dr. Guthrie because of the arthritis in her wrists, and only buys sliced bread now, because of the pain. She was in London on a very hot day and met her friend Ruth who works in television and Ruth introduced her to "these Enzensbergers," Ilse writes, probably members of a famous German family of intellectuals named Enzensberger, and in conversation with them, she says, she felt so different than with anyone else she usually spends time with. It seems like she didn't enjoy the Enzenbergers much. But maybe, she writes to Tom, this brush with actual Germans will help against that old blockade and allow her to write something about German-Jewish lives again.

∗ ∗ ∗ ∗ ∗

In 2007 her son, his second wife Ros, and Ilse's grandchildren are standing in front of a postwar building in Gaustraße, Bingen. On the pavement in front of the building are so-called "stepping stones:" memorials to deported and murdered Jews, three little golden squares bearing the names Bertha, Agnes, and Karl Gross. An old lady emerges from the house across the street. She asks Tom if he's a descendant of the family. When he says yes, she gives him a piece of paper. This, she says, she found on Gaustraße right after a bomb had destroyed the house in the war. She says she'd picked up that piece of paper and kept it all these years.

In 1900 one out of twelve Bingeners belonged to one of the two Jewish congregations. On September 21, 1905, the new reform synagogue opened in Rochusstraße. Flags decorated almost every building in the street. Thirty-three years later, Rochusstraße was "blocked with crowds," eyewitnesses said, with Bingeners "cheering loudly when the synagogue went up in flames." In 1900, there were 700 Jews living in Bingen. By the beginning of World War Two, the number had shrunk to 222, and three years later to 152. They were all deported to camps in 1942. Only two of the Jewish Bingeners who didn't emigrate survived the Holocaust.[11]

Tom looks at the glistening new memorial stones. He finds it slightly odd that they are located on the ground where people's feet will stomp on them. He thinks plaques at eye-level might work better.

His daughter Allegra is thirteen years old. His son Louis is ten, Here in Bingen the children learn that their grandmother's family had their own chauffeur: the driver of Gross & Sons. The grandma they knew had a red Clio and drove it herself. Allegra and Louis walk the streets of Bingen and they're a bit confused because there aren't just the stepping-stones in front of this one house, but many more stepping stones in front of all sorts of houses.

Tom looks at the piece of paper in his hand. Before 1935, a label like this one would be glued to wine bottles. The tag shows a view of Bingen: the Nahe flowing into the Rhine, church spires, Klopp Castle, Klopp Mountain. Over this panorama, words float: "W. Gross Söhne Bingen a. Rhein" and between "W. Gross Söhne" and "Bingen a. Rhein" sits the logo this Jewish German company used. It shows Saint Martin dividing his cloak.

⁕ ⁕ ⁕ ⁕ ⁕

Years later Ilse's grandchild Allegra is going to take courses in creative writing at the university. In these courses, she will write some poems about her grandmother. More time will pass until a biographer of Kathrine Talbot will ask Allegra to share these poems with him. She'll agree to his request and then never send them. At that point she's employed at a high-power London gallery, and she'll have a small window of time to go out for a coffee in her lunchbreak. On the day she meets the biographer, like every day, she will be wearing her great-grandmother's emerald ring.

Allegra remembers her grandmother's straight posture, her minimal make-up. Whenever her granddaughter spent the night, she couldn't just crawl into grandma's bed in the mornings. That was only possible with her other grandmother, the one they called "Nanny." Ilse was "Grandma." "Nanny" you could wrestle in the grass. Grandma Ilse brushed Allegra's hair, and that was about as intimate as things got.

Was she a cool woman? Maybe she was, if a cool woman would write to her granddaughter once a month, on her typewriter: a letter that always began with the words "Darling Allegra." She sent postcards to her other grandchild just as regularly: "Darling Louis." During a Zoom call years later, Louis will recall how, on these postcards, his grandma asked whether he was still feeding Mr. Jones' cows. That really was something he'd been doing for a while. The postcards to Louis showed animal motifs: sheep, zebras, giraffes. Ilse also writes to Frances, the other grandmother, "Nanny." One time, she writes: "I so wish I had your warmness, Frances."

⁕ ⁕ ⁕ ⁕ ⁕

Around the year 2000 a scholar named Alison Oldham investigates the art scene of postwar Cornwall. Conducting interviews with witnesses, Alison asks about gender roles. What were things like for women back then? How did it feel to work as a waitress or a hotel maid only so your male partner could have time to paint or write? When you yourself were a writer, a painter – and also needed time?

There's a poet wife of a male poet who feels insulted by Alison's question. Alison is belittling her, this woman says. She's judging her by today's standards. Another one of Alison's interviewees doesn't mind the question. Her name is Ilse Barker. Alison notes that it really was a matter of course for Ilse to take a step back behind Kit.[12] Ilse tells Alison that she is able to look back on a happy life, a life of many gifts, and that this witty, warm-hearted man, Kit Barker, was one of the greatest gifts she received.

In her role as Kathrine Talbot, Ilse goes back to Cornwall. In December 2002 she and Alison are doing a lecture tour there. In Penzance they have a large audience, standing room only. Alison presents her research. Ilse reads from *Kit Barker Cornwall 1947-1948*. Then they go to Mevagissey, just to take a look. It's peaceful in winter. The sea is magnificent. They drive north, to St. Ives, for the second and final gig on their tour. Not as many people. Then: Gurnard's Head, where one of Kit's works has been hanging on a pub wall for more than fifty years. The woman behind the counter tells Ilse how much the picture means to her. Maybe Ilse and Alison also stop by the little house close to Zennor, the one with the rain barrel, the one you could only reach with wet feet. Ilse stands in front of a fence there and wonders whether someone actually used spare parts from an old, noisy double bed to construct the gate right in front of her. But that could also be a scene from one of her new short stories. Kathrine Talbot never stops writing.[13]

* * * * *

She has made plans to move to Shropshire. It's where Tom and Ros live. Ilse is now eighty-five years old. The three of them have decided that it would be best to have Ilse live close by. She's supposed to move on Monday, May 22. Everything's sorted. On Sunday, May 21, she has a last lunch date in Sussex. Her friend Bronnie waits and waits. Ilse doesn't show up. That's unlike her.

This same day, May 21, Tom and Ros and Allegra and Louis are sitting in a car. They're taking a trip to the beach, to Aberystwyth. It's a ninety-minute drive. They haven't gone all that far when Bronnie calls Tom's mobile. Bronnie? They stop. Nine-year old Louis is sitting in the back of the car and has never seen his father cry before. But that's not the end of the story.

* * * * *

At the beginning of the memorial service, Bronnie reads a song by composer John Dowland, born in 1563. It's a song about weeping and grief and how sleep may bring peace. Then the actress Chloe Salaman reads a poem by Elizabeth Bishop. Chloe was Churchill's daughter Sarah in the series *Churchill* and Princess Elspeth in the film *Dragonslayer*. Her parents live at the foot of Bexley Hill. Salaman reads "One Art." The art in question is the art of learning how to lose: keys at first, then "your mother's watch," then rivers, cities, "a continent." The speaker lost all of these things. And a loved one, too. And "the joking voice" and "a gesture" which the speaker loved. "One Art" keeps stressing that losing wasn't a disaster. And then you notice the self-deception. Of course losing is a "disaster." Finally, the voice says not to push the pain away but to accept it, to *write it!*, as the printed version's last line says, in italics.

At the end of the reception a CD plays Bach, the "English Suite No. 2 in A Minor." Nobody has read from the work of writer Kathrine Talbot. Tom says he just didn't think it would have been what his mother wanted. It felt right the way it was.

* * * * *

About ten years later – this is how long it will take – Tom is going to have a dream that will seem utterly real. In it, his mother's sitting on a chair, in the center of a room, and he walks up to her and places his hand on her shoulder and asks her how she is. She says she's fine and she smiles. And this one isn't a dream: Whenever there's a British banknote in his hand, he thinks he sees his mother's face. But it's not. It's the face of the Queen.

* * * * *

After the service, a reception takes place in the Angel Hotel in Midhurst. People are hugging Tom, who, like his mother, isn't the hugging type. Noisy, emotional people have gathered here. Some are particularly noisy: that Irish poet, for instance (or is he Scottish?), and a number of Barkers from George's side of the family.

People give speeches. Julian Kent rises from his chair. He lives in Shropshire, just a few hills away from Tom. Until recently Tom had no idea Julian even existed. But when they were planning Ilse's move, his mother said how funny it was that she'd soon be living close to Julian. Julian? Well, the son of Howard Kent, the former Geoffrey Pittock-Buss, her first husband. It was the first time Tom heard about his mother's first marriage.[14]

It's getting louder at the Angel Hotel. Guests have a choice between white, red, and something that might be prosecco. Now there are spontaneous group hugs that really overtax Tom. So he has a glass and maybe a few more glasses after that, which means that he, the main person in charge here, doesn't have a clear sense of the afternoon he's in charge of. Progles Barker, a son of George, is the guest who seems the most drunk. And then the reception is over and there's so much cheese left that the staff at the Angel Hotel say to take the cheese, and then Ros drives the car the long way to Clun, which for the first few hours must have been the route of the train that deported Ilse in 1940, and later they drive through Shropshire and it's really late and the day was all a bit much.

* * * * *

Policemen broke down the door and found Ilse Barker dead in her bathtub. As is the way in such cases, investigations were made. Her death certificate says she died of drowning. It is dated May 20, 2006. Maybe she had a stroke, maybe a heart attack.

She'd always wanted to go to Switzerland. She wanted to see the mountains in springtime. She wanted to see the wildflowers.

The writer Anne Stevenson reads Ilse's obituary in the *Guardian* and sends a letter to Tom. She writes of how unsentimental his mother was. How free of self-pity. How one laughed with her about the terribleness of the world. Ilse was one of the most real people she knew.[15]

* * * * *

When Tom clears his mother's house, he finds manuscripts. There are poems, stories, and two autobiographical works, each about two hundred pages long. "Pompous" and "embarrassing:" these were the words Kathrine Talbot used when she referred to autobiographical writing. At some point she must have changed her mind. Because then, sandbags arrive on the streets and the food is rationed and a German-Jewish girl has managed to escape to England. Her parents haven't made it. There are barrage balloons floating over London, protecting the city from enemy aircraft.

This is the world which another pile of paper in Tom's hands takes him into: the pages of Kathrine Talbot's last unpublished novel. Unlike her other fiction, *Please Open the Door* doesn't portray charismatic bohemians, successful writers, affluent businessmen. Nor does it maintain the distance between fiction and reality. The German-Jewish girl, now working as a maid, is its heroine. The story is set in the winter of 1939/40. Finally Kathrine Talbot has turned her own life into a novel.

Anna, the German girl, works for an English couple. The husband heads a psychiatric hospital. In the house next to the hospital grounds, his wife is finding the new foreign maid unbearable. The doctor is having a secret affair with an occupational therapist. It won't be long until the relationship is no longer so secret. In this household, you're not supposed to have opinions. Having opinions isn't English. You're really not supposed to talk about anything. Saying the words "nine months" is considered vulgar, for instance, even if you weren't referring to a pregnancy at all, just something that lasted longer than eight and not as long as ten months. Also, you mustn't talk about the war, even though that's all everyone thinks about.

In Kathrine Talbot's first three novels, almost all protagonists are elegant and witty. Anna is different. After a year in England, she still doesn't know that "marmalade" has oranges in it whereas jam doesn't. She also can't do to her hair what English women do. And she's just as prude as her employers: She can't bear if someone mentions the county "Middlesex." Like Ilse Gross, however, she secretly reads Marie Stopes' *Married Love* and realizes that bodily intimacy doesn't have to be painful at all.

Anna's always hungry. She's always cold. She has chilblains. You know that something terrible is going to happen. And you don't have to wait long. In the kitchen, Anna is chopping oranges for marmalade. It's not jam. Keep that in mind. She needs to chop the fruit into very small pieces, the doctor's wife tells her, because the doctor really doesn't appreciate overly large pieces of rind in his marmalade (and he doesn't enjoy cooking smells in the house either, but he makes an exception where marmalade is concerned). Anna's chilblains hurt from the oranges' acid and there's a discussion about chopping methods which are either exactly correct or absolutely inacceptable, and then a knife falls to the floor and a door is opened and there's a knifing and blood and a tumultuous marital conflict and then the clumsy maid leaves this household behind and takes the train back to London, a city exposed to German bombs. In her train compartment, Anna sits sandwiched between English soldiers. She looks out the window onto a river. She sees swans on the water. She has no idea what's going to become of her. "A natural novelist."

11

The Portable Typewriter

When she was fourteen years old, after fleeing from Bingen, Ilse Gross moved to the pensionnat "Villa Sévigné" in a town called Pully, close to Lausanne, on Lake Geneva. Sixty years later, as Kathrine Talbot, she would write about this time in an autobiographical account. That report says that she read a lot of Rilke and Hofmannsthal back then. It mentions the portable typewriter her parents had given her before she left. And it states how important it had been to her, wherever she lived from now on, to encounter neither antisemites nor boys.

A Jewish boarding school for girls, Villa Sévigné must have seemed like the right place for her. She sat down at her typewriter. She typed her daily letter to her parents. And every day she would receive a reply. Her mother commented on Ilse's news and observations. She also listed spelling mistakes that her daughter had made. Her father just added a few lines. Her mother reminded Ilse to wash her hair and brush her teeth. Using colored crayons, Agnes Gross made drawings of Bingen. The bridge over the Nahe. Klopp Castle. In Pully Ilse took the drawings from the envelopes.

The two Mademoiselles Bloch – Blanche and Mathilde – ran the pensionnat. Mathilde Bloch had just received the Palme d'Or for her achievements in teaching French literature and culture.[1] Her new student, her French less than mediocre, felt a dark and crippling homesickness and yet wrote cheerful letters to Bingen.

Ilse kept crying. She couldn't stop. She hated life in the villa so much. But she also knew what her parents were going through. Her father was closing down the family business, which had been going since 1835. And it was routine in Bingen's everyday life to humiliate Jews on the street. Because she knew this, she wrote to her parents that everything was just dandy in Pully. Every day she took a new sheet of paper, turned the carriage of the typewriter, pushed the lever that made the carriage move all the way to the right. And then she wrote fiction about her wonderful new life at boarding school.

All the other girls talked about were boys, clothes, and patisserie. She couldn't take walks on her own; you always had to walk in group formation.

In Bingen she had always taken solitary walks, up and down the hills, through the vineyards to the left and right. Here she was just steps from Lake Geneva. She could have looked at the water, the clouds, and Evian on the other side of the lake, eight miles away. But they made her stay inside.

In the winter the pensionnat relocated to Champéry, in the Valais. Here were the Dents de Midi and the Dents Blanches, mountains almost two miles high. Skiing was a nightmare. She had no talent whatsoever. If you used the bathroom in the cabin, everyone could hear every little sound your body made. And it turned out that most of the other girls, Swiss, French, English, didn't really want to spend time with a German girl. In Germany Jews were being persecuted and now those who weren't German seemed to think that the German Jews had only themselves to blame. Yet Ilse's parents had worries that were so much more pressing.

One of Ilse's teachers in Pully commented that Ilse had "a tendency toward "melancholia." The events in Germany, this educator wrote, left a "strong influence on her thoughts." For months Ilse wrote cheerful letters to Bingen, until she finally got up the courage to say that she couldn't bear the Villa Sévigné any longer. Her parents rearranged things. In June 1936, fifteen years old, she left Pully for a new institution, an hour away, in Chataigneriaz, toward the narrow end of the lake.

"The students are surrounded by loving diligence," the advertisement brochure for her new school read. "Nonetheless Frau Dr. Rittmeyer reserves the right to reprimand." Ilse could have learned cooking, baking, and preserving from Dr. Rittmeyer, and gardening, poultry farming, washing, ironing, sewing. In September, though, she moved on to Geneva.

There she lived on the same lake and in a different universe. She was a student at what is now known as "Ecolint," the first international school on this planet, founded just twelve years earlier, a cosmopolitan educational experiment for a future that one could only expect to be peaceful. Everything was simpler here, and freer. She could read and write, spend time alone. Take walks by herself. There was always music playing somewhere. Chopin. When the school theatre group performed *Hamlet*, she played Guildenstern.

She managed to grow accustomed to what she'd been afraid of: male company. She did, however, decline a marriage proposal. She photographed Mr. Dean and Mr. Stump in Geneva, youthful teachers of hers. When Dean and Stump played basketball, Ilse had the camera ready. A distinct linguistic confusion seems to have grasped her, along with a significant interest in Mr. Dean's activities. "Dean spealt Basqued," she noted underneath a picture she pasted into a photo album. "Dean macht ein gaul" beneath another one.

She photographed the girls and – more frequently – the boys in her school. Some wore ties and jackets, some sports uniforms, some lay in the sun, some had books under their arms, a trophy in their hand or a razor on their cheek. One of her Jewish schoolmates would later enter the liberated concentration camp Buchenwald, the first allied officer to walk through the gates. His name was Edward Tenenbaum and she might have photographed him as well.[2]

* * * * *

Around Easter 1938, her parents were planning to come for a visit to Geneva. But it was hard for them to get travel permits. That spring Ilse played a music teacher in the school play, in Alfred de Musset's *On ne badine pas avec l'amour*. She wore a dress coat and large men's shoes. Someone painted a black moustache underneath her nose. Before the show started, she was called to the phone. Her mother had arrived. Because Alfred de Musset hadn't made the music teacher very significant, Ilse was free to leave during the break. She ran over to the hotel, through the long hallway, in her clunky shoes, and then stood before her mother who had heard the heavy steps coming closer and who now stared at this moustache. Hugs. Kisses. Laughter. And much of the moustache was left on her mother's face.

After a few mother-daughter-days, after hot chocolate and whipped cream in the park La Perle du Lac and after watching the movie *A Hundred Men and A Girl* – a masterpiece, no question about it –, her father arrived. He had a travel permit for three weeks. And they went off together. Three of the four members of the Gross family spent their holiday in a Lugano hotel. Again and again, they sat on a steamer cruising over the lake.

On one occasion, Ilse got off the lift in the hotel lobby, seventeen years old, in a long ballgown, a red carnation at her décolleté, and looked at her father sitting there, in one of the comfortable armchairs, reading a paper, smoking a cigar. His hair seemed to be either still blonde or already grey. His moustache was clearly still blonde. He seemed content in this moment, his daughter thought.

Ilse wanted to go dancing. And her parents made that possible, night after night. She had a sister who couldn't dance and whom her parents would probably never be able to leave behind. During one of the hotel balls Ilse won a prize for a waltz danced with an English medical student. It was a toy giraffe. Then the Easter holidays were over. Her mother would accompany her to Geneva. The father changed trains in Lausanne. They embraced and they kissed. He stayed on the platform as Ilse and her mother departed. He took off his cap and took the cigar from his mouth. He smiled. He lifted his cap. He waved.

✴ ✴ ✴ ✴ ✴

Kathrine Talbot wrote these scenes more than half a century after they had taken place. For a very long time she'd been unable to write about her memories. And then she succeeded.

From our vantage point we could see this as a major breakthrough. In our time, autobiographical writing is even more popular than in Kathrine Talbot's – and the closeness between literary texts and experienced life has become a major selling point on the book market.[3] If this was a breakthrough, though, it certainly came too late to make her oeuvre more successful. Except for her Cornwall booklet, her autobiographical texts were never published. Nor was the novel *Please Open the Door*, in which she had found the most straightforward way to turn her wartime experiences into fiction.

In Kathrine Talbot's published works, *Fire in the Sun, The Innermost Cage*, and *Return,* some critics saw a lack of substance, action, and plot. They praised her style and complained about a lack of drama. They detected artificiality, people's suffering implausibly evoked. And we can now see the irony in this. The author who didn't seem to provide enough authentic tragedy had immensely tragic 'material' at her disposal. She could have told the story of persecution in Bingen: her hometown as a microcosm of intimacy and violence, with the surreal, idyllic backdrop of the vineyards on the hills. She could have built a novel around her parents' dilemma. Should they escape from Germany with one of their daughters – or remain to protect the other one? Or she could have written about her own breakdown, her escape, her internment, her grief. She waited too long.

Like so many other people, Ilse Gross/Ilse Barker/Kathrine Talbot responded to the Holocaust with silence.[4] Anyone wondering why this young woman didn't rush to produce an autobiographical work about her family's experiences would ignore how profoundly persecution and exile disturbed all forms of literary expression – and particularly traditional forms of biographical prose. All autobiographical writing departs from the notion that protagonists are independent people who set the course of their own existence. These concepts were destroyed first in the reality of Nazi Germany.[5]

Kathrine Talbot may have looked to fiction to find freedom. Certainly, though, she was less free than other authors. There's German author W.G. Sebald, twenty years younger than she and not a Jew. He was raised in Bavaria and taught in England. Around the millennium, Sebald produced one of the most refined and successful novels of the "postmemory" period. *Austerlitz* circles around Theresienstadt and the experiences of young Jewish refugees in Britain. At one point in the novel, Sebald's protagonist, now an adult, having been saved by the Kindertransport, his parents killed by the Germans, finds himself on a train going down the Rhine. He sees Bingen. He looks at the Mouse Tower and thinks that in the Rhine Valley it's impossible to say "what era you're living in." To Jewish refugee Ilse Barker, the former Ilse Gross, a real person, not an imagined protagonist, another historical "era" was so painfully present on the Rhine that she quickly walked back to the car and escaped from Bingen a second time. She lacked the emotional distance that allowed W.G. Sebald to turn *Austerlitz* into such nuanced prose. Because she felt the pain, she couldn't tell its story.[6]

* * * * *

In the spring of 1938 Ilse saw her father for the last time; in late summer of 1938, her mother. For several years, her parents and her sister continued to live under Nazi rule. A few months after saying goodbye to their younger daughter in Switzerland and returning to Germany, the freedoms and human rights of Karl and Agnes Gross were drastically limited. Following the November pogroms, various laws that excluded Jews from public spaces were passed in quick succession. These measures, historian Saul Friedländer points out, were the first indications that Jews would be concentrated spatially in the future.[7]

On April 30, 1942, Ilse's sister Bertha was deported to Poland, along with around one hundred other patients and staff of a Jewish psychiatric clinic in Bendorf-Sayn near Koblenz. The train left Koblenz and, after four days, arrived in Krasnystaw, Lublin. The deported were housed in the ghetto Krasniczyn. This ghetto was vacated a few weeks later. The Germans shot two hundred individuals on the Krasniczyn graveyard. The other ghetto inhabitants were taken to Belzec and Sobibor death camps. It is unknown how long Bertha Gross survived after leaving the clinic in Bendorf-Sayn.[8]

On September 27, 1942, Ilse's parents Karl and Agnes Gross were deported from Darmstadt, near Frankfurt, to Theresienstadt. Karl's death from starvation there, on February 1, 1944, was a typical form of dying. As in all German ghettos and camps, most of the Theresienstadt inmates suffered from malnutrition. In the everyday lives of the inmates this also meant that the older they were, the less food was available to them. Karl Gross was sixty-four in the winter of 1943/44. Because they needed more calories per day, men died more quickly of malnutrition than women.[9]

After her husband's death, Agnes Gross survived Theresienstadt for eight more months. On June 23, 1944, delegates from the International Red Cross and the Danish government visited the camp. They departed with the erroneous belief that they had seen an autonomous Jewish town and not a transit institution that was part of a death camp system. On October 7, 1944, German bureaucrats scheduled Agnes Gross for the transport to Auschwitz on the following day. Measures exempting Jewish war veterans and their relatives had been recalled. The train left Terezín a day late, on October 9, a Jewish holiday: Simchat Tora, "Rejoicing with – or of – the Torah." There were 1,600 children and adults on the train. It reached Birkenau on October 12. Because of Agnes Gross' age – she had just turned sixty-one – it must be assumed that she was killed in a gas chamber upon arrival.[10]

Perhaps Kathrine Talbot's concerns about her German-Jewish 'material' were also craft-related issues, in a traditional journalistic sense. Even in Pully, a fourteen-year-old girl sitting at her brand-new portable typewriter, she must have had a clear sense of the distinct difference between fiction and nonfiction. Later on, she was able to portray her parents only in the manner in which she had encountered them: as free people, making their own decisions. She couldn't write about their experiences between 1938 and 1944. In an autobiographical text she noted how the suffering of her family had been "locked away" from her for decades. She tried to imagine how her parents must have felt and thought. And it didn't work out. At some point, though, she did write about saying good-bye.

* * * * *

After taking her degree in the summer of 1938, seventeen-year-old Ilse moved out of the International School and into a small Geneva pension.

She took French classes at the university. Ice cream was excellent in Geneva: green pistachio or peach. She had friends from Scandinavia, from Argentina. They went swimming during the day and dancing at night.

Her father was unable to get a travel permit that summer. But her mother, Agnes Gross, succeeded. She moved into Ilse's room at the pension. They saw the branches of a linden tree right outside the window. They took walks in the city. They sat in cafés. In the evenings Agnes Gross had a glass of beer. She said it helped against her sleeplessness.

Her mother, Ilse noticed, still had slender hands and pretty ankles. She wore a black straw hat with a bright red band around it. Ilse was proud of her mother's beauty and the attentive way she studied people. Sometimes Ilse left her mother alone, met with friends, and then she returned and told her mother all the details of her evening. They didn't talk much about the future. There was no way of predicting it. "When we're together again." That was a phrase they said a lot.

Some days they spoke French with each other. Ilse found a special joy in correcting her mother's mistakes. She took her mother to her favorite spot in all of Geneva. It must have been – her account isn't entirely clear here – somewhere in the Parc des Bastions, with a view of the Grand Théâtre. Late in the afternoon it was prettiest there, the light golden and dusty.

On the day her mother departed for Bingen, they went to a restaurant close to the station, on Place de Cornavin. They ordered soup. Approximately six decades later, Ilse Barker in Midhurst, Sussex, placed her fingers on a computer keyboard and wrote that she still remembered the taste, the consistency, and the color of that chicken consommé. A bit thin, pale yellow, with an egg in it. A rather lukewarm soup, very mild, like soup you serve sick people if you want to help them recover.

They paid and they left. The mother said it wasn't nice to say goodbye in the train station. It seemed too sad, she said. They hugged on the square.

About This Book

I could only write this book because Ilse Barker's son Tom replied to an e-mail by an unknown German in November 2019 – and after that, continued to respond to numerous additional e-mails, text messages, calls, and video interview invitation links. Later on, he sent packages, fed his mother's biographer, drove him around Shropshire, drove all the way to Bingen to meet him there, and brought a magnificent painting of two sheep along. I am tremendously grateful to Tom and Ros Barker.

Most of the details of this narrative are drawn from Kathrine Talbot's/Ilse Barker's nonfictional texts: her unpublished autobiographical works written around the turn of the 21st century ("The Painted Tides" and "The Cuckoo under the Chair") and her memoir of the Cornwall years (*Kit Barker Cornwall 1947-1948: Recollections of Painters and Writers*). In contrast, I treated her novels and short stories as fictional texts and took the greatest care not to misunderstand them as representations of their author's reality. As additional sources I used poems, letters, diaries, notes, and pictures from Ilse Barker's papers. I also depended on the letters Elizabeth Bishop sent to Kit and Ilse Barker between 1952 and 1979. The original correspondence is housed in the Princeton University Library (Special Collections).

While it is true that the memories and observations of author Kathrine Talbot constitute the backbone of this book's material, my narrative of her life differs significantly from her autobiographical texts (which often centered on other people: her husband, her parents). I emphasize some aspects of her life and make others seem less important. This is particularly true for Kit Barker's paintings and his career as an artist. These matters were highly relevant to Ilse Barker and had to be relegated to the background here to make room for Kathrine Talbot's literary work.

I did follow her notes, though, instead of speculating about what was going on in her mind. To cite an example: When young Ilse Gross, after her arrival in London, is saddened because there's the "wrong" kind of tablecloth before her, this appears in her written work and doesn't result from my speculations that her grandfather's tablecloth company might have prompted such an emotional reaction in his granddaughter. I only referred to observations and emotions when I saw them documented in her nonfictional work.

To fill gaps, I conducted interviews with witnesses and experts. Again, I need to thank Tom and Ros Barker – and Allegra Nancini-Barker, Sue Nancini-Barker, and Louis Nancini-Barker. I am very grateful to Beate Goetz in Bingen, who got me started on this project. Esther Fairfax took time for a conversation about her friend Ilse. Julian and Jane Kent reported from the point of view of Geoffrey Pittock-Buss's family. Giles Halliwell shared memories of Bexley Hill. Alison Oldham read the manuscript, answered lots of questions, and enriched this book as Ilse Barker's friend and as an expert of the postwar Cornwall art scene. I found fabulous experts at the University of Southampton: Jennifer Craig-Norton, Tony Kushner, and Joachim Schloer. Andrea Hammel (University of Aberystwyth) provided much-needed help. Lori Gemeiner Bihler (Framingham State University) answered questions about how to do German Jewish refugee history. I am very grateful to Elise Bath (Wiener Library) for sending important information my way. Thomas Travisano (Hartwick College) helped in Elizabeth Bishop matters and with so much more. Sue Vice (University of Sheffield) graciously supported this book. Stephen Prince talked about postwar Cornwall. Dean Rogers (Vassar College) supplied Bishop-Barker documents. Herbert Baaser answered questions about Bingen wine. Sarah Christian and Kim Holden (Manx National Heritage) helped my research about internment on the Isle of Man.

In Switzerland let me thank Alejandro Rodriguez-Giovo (International School of Geneva) for his generous contributions to my research. Additional help regarding Ilse Gross' years in Switzerland came from: Alain Dubois (Archives d'Etat de Genève), Marcel Ruegg (Archives de la Ville de Lausanne), Mathieu Saboureau (Archives Communales, Ville de Pully), Caroline Bertron (Université Paris-Dauphine), Lea Haller and Daniel DiFalco (*NZZ Geschichte*), René Loeb (Schweizerische Vereinigung für Jüdische Genealogie), Bernard Bertoncini (Commune de Coppet), and Sylviane Javet and Yannick Cohen (Communauté Israelite de Lausanne et du Canton de Vaude). Caspar Battegay (University of Basel) took time to discuss terminology with me.

Thanks also go out to: Ilse Ribbat and Ernst Ribbat, Richard Grasshoff, Farid Salih, Sandra Jansen, Alexandra Hartmann, Denise Parkinson (superb reader of blurbs), to research assistants at the University of Paderborn (Maike Doll, Jan Fieseler, Miriam Jaßmeier, Meher Malik, Angelina Morad, and Marie Smith), and to Petra Meyenbrock. Thank you, Jamie Lee Searle, for your excellent editing.

Finally, I would like to express my admiration for Ilse Gross, Ilse Pittock-Buss, Kathrine Pittock, Ilse Barker, Kathrine Talbot. I learned a lot from her: about literature, writing, letters, and life in general. Reading an article about Elizabeth Bishop, I came across her name – one of her names – in a footnote. Beate Goetz in Bingen then relayed me to Thomas Barker, wonderful artist and person. And finally let me recommend a pub in Shropshire. When visiting her son Tom in Clun, Ilse Barker enjoyed having a half pint of bitter at the White Horse. It's not so long ago.

Endnotes

CHAPTER 1

1   For sources from the Ilse Barker/Kathrine Talbot Papers and information drawn from interviews with witnesses and experts, see the chapter "About This Book." For the coded hanging of laundry as a potential signal for German planes: M. Kochan, "Women's Experience of Internment," in D. Cesarani and T. Kushner (eds.), *The Internment of Aliens in Twentieth Century Britain* (London: Frank Cass, 1993), pp. 147-188.

CHAPTER 2

1   B. Bernard, "Tourismus in Bingen in den 1930er Jahren," in M. Schmandt (ed.), *Bingen im Nationalsozialismus: Quellen und Studien* (Bad Kreuznach: Matthias Ess, 2018), pp. 211-261.

2   N. Brunnhuber, *The Faces of Janus: English-Language Fiction by German-Speaking Exiles in Great Britain, 1933-45* (Oxford: Peter Lang, 2005), pp. 16-21.

3   W. Strickhausen, "Großbritannien," in C. Krohn et al. (eds.), *Handbuch der deutschsprachigen Emigration, 1933-1945* (Darmstadt: Wissenschaftliche Buchgesellschaft, 2012), pp. 251-270.

4   L. Segal, *Other People's Houses* (1964) (London: Sort Of Books, 2018), p. 7.

5   For critical discussions of the Kindertransport see: A. Hammel and B. Lewkowicz (eds.), *The Kindertransport to Britain 1938/39: New Perspectives* (Amsterdam: Rodopi, 2012); C. McDonald, "'We Became British Aliens:' Kindertransport Refugees Narrating the Discovery of their Parents' Fates," *Holocaust Studies* 24, 4 (2018), pp. 395-417; T. Kushner, "The Big Kindertransport Myth," *The Jewish Chronicle* (November 15, 2018), https://www.thejc.com/news/features/the-big-kindertransport-myth-kindertransport80th-anniversary-1.472542 (accessed August 3, 2023); J. Craig-Norton, *The Kindertransport: Contesting Memory* (Bloomington: Indiana University Press, 2019).

6   E. Klee, *"Euthanasie" im Dritten Reich: Die "Vernichtung lebensunwerten Lebens"* (Frankfurt am Main: Fischer, 2014); R. Forsbach, "'Euthanasie' und Zwangssterilisierungen im Rheinland (1933-1945)," *Portal Rheinische Geschichte* (2017), https://www.rheinische-geschichte.lvr.de/themen (accessed August 3, 2023).

7   J. Craig-Norton, "Refugees at the Margins: Jewish Domestics in Britain, 1938-1945," *Shofar* 37, 3 (2019), pp. 295-330; R. Göpfert, *Der jüdische Kindertransport von Deutschland nach England 1938/39: Geschichte und Erinnerung* (Frankfurt am Main: Campus, 1999), pp. 176-177. In a few cases married couples succeeded in acquiring visas, if they both worked in one and the same household. See: T. Bollauf, *Dienstmädchen-Emigration: Die Flucht jüdischer Frauen aus Österreich und Deutschland nach England 1938/39* (Vienna: LIT, 2011), p. 162.

8   E. Nesbit, *The Wouldbegoods: Being the Further Adventures of the Treasure Seekers* (1901) (Harmondsworth: Penguin, 1971), p. 151.

9   T. Bollauf, *Dienstmädchen-Emigration*, p. 213.

10 C. Brinson, "A Woman's Place...? German-Speaking Women in Exile in Britain, 1933-1945," in *German Life and Letters* 51, 2 (April 1998), pp. 204-224; J. Craig-Norton, "Refugees at the Margins;" L. Bihler, *Cities of Refuge: German Jews in London and New York, 1935-1945* (Albany: State University of New York Press, 2019), p. 67, pp. 109-110; T. Kushner, "An Alien Occupation: Jewish Refugees and Domestic Service in Britain, 1933-1948," in W. Mosse (ed.), *Second Chance: Two Centuries of German-Speaking Jews in the United Kingdom* (Tübingen: Mohr, 1991) pp. 553-578.

11 C. Morgan, *The Flashing Stream* (Rome: The Albatross, 1949). Opening night on September 1, 1938; Godfrey Tearle played mathematician Edward Ferrers and Margaret Rawlings his colleague Karen Selby (Morgan, p. 48).

12 W. Mayer-Gross, "Zur Phänomenologie abnormer Glücksgefühle," in *Zeitschrift für Pathopsychologie* 2 (1914), pp. 588-610.

13 *Mistress and Maid: General Information for the Use of Domestic Refugees and Their Employers* (London: The Domestic Bureau, Central Office for Refugees, 1940).

14 M. Stopes, *Married Love or Love in Marriage* (1918) (Oxford: Oxford University Press, 2004).

15 K. Grahame, *The Wind in the Willows* (1908) (London: Hamlyn, 1989).

16 Thousands of German and Austrian maids were let go by their employers when the war began. Ilse Gross was lucky. See: Kushner, "An Alien Occupation," p. 573.

CHAPTER 3

1   D. Moule et al., *Friend or Foe? The Fascinating Story of Women's Internment during WW II in Port Erin & Port St. Mary, Isle of Man* (Douglas: Rushen Heritage Trust, 2018), pp. 78-79.

2   Moule et al., *Friend or Foe?*, pp. 17-19; J.M. Ritchie, "German Refugees from Nazism," in P. Panayi (ed.), *Germans in Britain Since 1500* (London: Bloomsbury, 1996), pp. 147-170.

3   M. Kochan, "Women's Experience of Internment."

4   On these and other interned women: C. Brinson, "Introduction," in Ruth Borchard, *We Are Strangers Here: An 'Enemy Alien' in Prison in 1940* (London: Vallentine Mitchell, 2008), pp. 1-15.

5   Moule et al., *Friend or Foe?*, p. 189; p. 204.

6   Bihler, *Cities of Refuge*, p. 32.

7   F. Uhlman, *The Making of an Englishman* (London: Victor Gollancz, 1960), p. 241.

8   C. Chappell, *Island of Barbed Wire: Internment on the Isle of Man in World War Two* (London: Robert Hale, 1984), p. 89.

9   R. Michaelis-Jena, *Auch wir waren des Kaisers Kinder: Lebenserinnerungen* (Lemgo: Wagener, 1985), p. 142.

10   Kochan, "Women's Experience of Internment," p. 157.

11   Moule et al., *Friend or Foe?*, p. 79.

12   Ibid., p. 97.

13   Brinson, "A Womans Place...?," p. 212; another study mentions three newspapers in the women's camp: *Frauenruf, Rushen Outlook* and *Awful Times*. See: M. Seyfert, *Im Niemandsland: Deutsche Exilliteratur in britischer Internierung: Ein unbekanntes Kapitel der Kulturgeschichte des Zweiten Weltkriegs* (Berlin: Arsenal, 1984), p. 60.

14   Camp librarian Ruth Michaelis-Jena ran a bookstore in Detmold, Germany, until it was disfigured by antisemitic slogans in 1933. She worked as a bookseller in Edinburgh until she was called before the tribunal. See her autobiography: Michaelis-Jena, *Auch wir waren des Kaisers Kinder.*

15   This was observed by internee Eva Meyerhof, who used a pen name to publish a 1942 nonfiction account of her time in the woman's camp: L. Laurent, *A Tale of Internment* (London: Allen & Unwin, 1942), pp. 86-89.

16   In her autobiographical writings Kathrine Talbot mentions that she earned and spent money on the Isle of Man. There were periods, though, when the use of money was declared illegal in the women's camp. Interned economist Ruth Borchard developed a "service exchange scheme," in which a voucher system for services rendered replaced the circulation of money (Brinson, "A Woman's Place...?," p. 212).

17   F. Ford, *The March of Literature: From Confucius to Modern Times* (1939) (London: Allen & Unwin, 1947), p. 438. In spite of the subtitle Ford did begin with an exploration of ancient Egyptian literature.

18   Ford, *The March of Literature*, p. 768.

19   J. White, *London in the Twentieth Century: A City and Its People* (London: Vintage, 2001), pp. 38-39; Uhlman, *The Making of an Englishman*, p. 240.

20   K.D. Goldberg, "Wie der Wein in Mitteleuropa jüdisch wurde," in A. Lehnardt (ed.), *Wein und Judentum*, (Berlin: Neofelis, 2014), pp. 229-246.

21   G. Herbert, "The Affliction (I)," in H. Wilcox (ed.), *The English Poems of George Herbert* (Cambridge: Cambridge UP, 2007), pp. 162-3.

22   Kochan, *Women's Experience of Internment*, p. 161.

23   L. Laurent, *A Tale of Internment*, p. 93.

24   K. Diamant, *Kafka's Last Love: The Mystery of Dora Diamant* (London: Secker & Warburg, 2003), p. 232.

CHAPTER 4

1   Bihler, *Cities of Refuge*, p. 82.

2   R. Hewison, *Under Siege: Literary Life in London 1939-1945* (London: Weidenfeld and Nicolson, 1977), p. 49.

3   Hewison, *Under Siege*, pp. 33-36.

4   White, *London in the Twentieth Century*, p. 39 (in these passages White cites observations by writer Elizabeth Bowen).

5   V. Brittain, *Seed of Chaos: What Mass Bombing Really Means* (London: New Vision, 1944); Richard Rempel, "The Dilemmas of British Pacifists During World War II," in *The Journal of Modern History* 50, 4 (1978), pp. D1213-D1229.

6   A. Huxley, *Ends and Means: An Enquiry into the Nature of Ideals and into the Methods Employed for Their Realization* (1937) (London: Chatto & Windus, 1980), pp. 124-125.

7   For the reaction of emigré intellectual Siegfried Kracauer to the flow of information concerning the extermination of European Jews, see: J. Später, *Siegfried Kracauer: Eine Biographie* (Berlin: Suhrkamp, 2016), pp. 445-447.

8   T. Tanner, "Introduction," in T. Tanner (ed.), *Henry James* (London: MacMillan, 1968), pp. 11-41; H. James, *The Sacred Fount* (1901) (New York: Grove, 1979), p. 31, pp. 82-83.

9   H. James, "The Art of Fiction" (1884), in L. Edel (ed.), Henry James, *Major Stories and Essays* (New York: Library of America, 1999), pp. 572-593.

10 J. Gardiner, *Wartime: Britain 1939-1945* (London: Headline, 2004), p. 350.

11 Gardiner, *Wartime*, pp. 572-573.

12   T. Kushner, "The Holocaust in the British Imagination: The Official Mind and Beyond, 1945 to the Present," in *Holocaust Studies* 23, 3 (2017), pp. 1-21; Kushner, "From 'This Belsen Business' to 'Shoah Business': History, Memory, and Heritage, 1945-2005," in S. Bardgett and D. Cesarani (eds.), *Belsen 1945: New Historical Perspectives* (London: Vallentine Mitchell, 2006), pp. 189-216.

13   H. Green, *Loving* (1945) (London: Harvill, 1992), pp. 70-71.

14   K. Friedlander, *The Psycho-Analytical Approach to Juvenile Delinquency: Theory, Case-Studies, Treatment* (London: Kegan Paul, Trench, Trubner, 1947), pp. 14-15; pp. 286-287.

15   For a study of "language change" in emigré writing, here in the case of author Klaus Mann, see: S. Utsch, *Sprachwechsel im Exil: Die "linguistische Metamorphose" von Klaus Mann* (Cologne: Böhlau, 2007); for a range of other exiled Jewish writers in the German-British context (most of them much older than Ilse Gross) see: D. Vietor-Engländer, "What's in a Name? What Is Jewishness? New Definitions for Two Generations: Elsa Bernstein, Anna Gmeyner, Ruth Ewald, and Others," in M. Gelber, J. Hessing and R. Jütte (eds.), *Integration und Ausgrenzung: Studien zur deutsch-jüdischen Literatur- und Kulturgeschichte von der Frühen Neuzeit bis zur Gegenwart* (Tübingen: Max Niemeyer, 2009), pp. 467-481.

16   W. Allen, "Henry Green," in *Penguin New Writing* (London: Penguin, 1945), pp. 144-155.

17   A. Robinson, *The Bleak Midwinter 1947* (Manchester: Manchester University Press, 1987).

18   G. Viney, *The Last Hurrah: The 1947 Royal Tour of Southern Africa and the End of Empire* (London: Robinson, 2019).

CHAPTER 5

1   D. Cesarani, "Great Britain," in D. Wyman and C. Rosenzweig (eds.), *The World Reacts to the Holocaust* (Baltimore: Johns Hopkins University Press, 1996), pp. 599-641; T. Kushner, *The Holocaust and the Liberal Imagination: A Social and Cultural History* (Oxford: Blackwell, 1994), pp. 205-269; contrasting the claim that complete silence had reigned regarding the Holocaust up until the 1960s, a more nuanced reading insists that Holocaust representations in the immediate postwar years were indeed visible, however marginalized they might have been. See: D. Cesarani and E. Sundquist (eds.), *After the Holocaust: Challenging the Myth of Silence* (London: Routledge, 2012). For a far-reaching exploration of the historical and cultural framework see: T. Lawson and A. Pearce (eds.), *The Palgrave Handbook of Britain and the Holocaust* (London: Palgrave, 2020).

2   R. Sullivan, *By Heart: Elizabeth Smart. A Life* (New York: Viking, 1991), pp. 157-162.

3   C. Barker, *The Arms of the Infinite* (Hebden Bridge: Pomona, 2006), p. 8; the turbulent relationship between Elizabeth Smart and George Barker prompted a widely read memoir by Smart. See: E. Smart, *By Grand Central Station I Sat Down and Wept* (1945) (London: Fourth Estate, 2015).

4   R. Fraser, *The Chameleon Poet: A Life of George Barker* (London: Jonathan Cape, 2001), p. 262.

5   Cesarani, "Great Britain;" T. Kushner, "Anti-Semitism and Austerity: The August 1947 Riots in Britain," in P. Panayi (ed.), *Racial Violence in Britain, 1840-1950* (London: Leicester University Press, 1996), pp. 150-170.

6   F. Bryan, "Rosamunde Pilcher Obituary," *The Guardian* (February 7, 2019), https://www.theguardian.com/books/2019/feb/07/rosamunde-pilcher-obituary (accessed August 9, 2023); *Rosamunde Pilcher Drehorte*, http://pilcher-drehorte.blogspot.com/ (accessed August 9, 2023); S. Bublitz (ed.), *The World of Rosamunde Pilcher* (New York: St. Martin's, 1996).

7   D. Kynaston, *Austerity Britain 1945-1951* (London: Bloomsbury, 2007), pp. 103-109.

CHAPTER 6

1   For the gendered New York art world in this time see: M. Brennan, *Modernism's Masculine Subjects: Matisse, The New York School, and Post-Painterly Abstraction* (Cambridge: MIT Press, 2004) and M. Gabriel, *Ninth Street Women: Lee Krasner, Elaine de Kooning, Grace Hartigan, Joan Mitchell, and Helen Frankenthaler: Five Painters and the Movement that Changed Modern Art* (New York: Little Brown, 2018).

2   C. Lupton, *Reading and the Making of Time in the Eighteenth Century* (Baltimore: Johns Hopkins University Press, 2018), pp. 38-42.

3   M. Brenson, "Jimmy Ernst, Painter, Dies; Emphasized Color and Line," *New York Times* (February 7, 1984), D 24, https://www.nytimes.com/1984/02/07/obituaries/jimmy-ernst-painter-dies-emphasized-color-and-line.html (accessed August 23, 2023).

4   For this picture agency's history and significance see: H. Neubauer, *Black Star: 60 Years of Photojournalism* (Cologne: Könemann, 1997).

5   For the career of Willy Mayer-Gross: C. Greenland, "At the Crichton Royal with William Mayer-Gross," in *History of Psychiatry* 13 (2002), pp. 467-474; regarding insulin shock therapy see: J. Braslow, *Mental Ills and Bodily Cures: Psychiatric Treatment in the First Half of the Twentieth*

Century (Berkeley: University of California Press, 1997), pp. 96-99. Willy Mayer-Gross' son Henry became an ornithologist and produced a magisterial work on the correct observation methods of bird's nests, based on 20,000 bird nest observation cards filled in by British ornithologists. See: H. Mayer-Gross, *Nest Record Scheme* (Beech Grove: British Trust for Ornithology, 1970).

6   V. Woolf, *A Room of One's Own* (London: Hogarth Press, 1929), p. 6.

7   B. Bernard, "'...alles war beschmutzt und besudelt': Das Judenpogrom in Bingen und die Zerstörung der Binger Synagogen am 10. November 1938," in M. Schmandt (ed.), *Bingen im Nationalsozialismus: Quellen und Studien* (Bad Kreuznach: Matthias Ess, 2018), pp. 303-359.

8   C. Boggess, *James Still: A Life* (Lexington: University Press of Kentucky, 2017), p. 243.

9   W. Cannella, "Writing Back: An Arbitrary History: Ilse Barker's Correspondence with Elizabeth Bishop," unpublished and undated manuscript, Boston College. Found in the Ilse Barker/Kathrine Talbot Papers.

10   University of Iowa, "Guide to the Calvin Kentfield Papers," https://aspace.lib.uiowa.edu/repositories/2/resources/583 (accessed August 16, 2023).

CHAPTER 7

1   IBM, "Installation of the first 701" (1953), in *IBM Archives* (undated), https://www.ibm.com/ibm/history/exhibits/701/701_first.html (accessed August 9, 2023).

2   E. Black, *IBM and the Holocaust: The Strategic Alliance between Nazi Germany and America's Most Powerful Corporation* (2001) (New York: Dialog, 2012).

3   H. Rodenberg, *The Making of Ernest Hemingway: Celebrity, Photojournalism, and the Emergence of the Modern Lifestyle Media* (Münster: LIT, 2014).

4   M. McGurl, *The Program Era: Postwar Fiction and the Rise of Creative Writing* (Cambridge: Harvard University Press, 2009), p. 61.

CHAPTER 8

1   G. Nugent, "Obituaries: Viscount Cowdray," *The Independent* (January 21, 1995), https://www.independent.co.uk/news/people/obituaries-viscount-cowdray-1568971.html (accessed August 9, 2023); W. Saxon, "Lord Cowdray, 84, Developer of the Pearson Conglomerate," *New York Times* (January 21, 1995), https://www.nytimes.com/1995/01/21/

obituaries/lord-cowdray-84-developer-of-the-pearson-conglomerate.html (accessed August 9, 2023).

2   C. Richmond, "Leslie Baruch Brent Obituary," *The Guardian* (January 2, 2020), https://www.theguardian.com/science/2020/jan/02/leslie-baruch-brent-obituary (accessed August 9, 2023); E. Sulis Gear, "The Nobel-Prize Winning Academic Who Fled Nazi Germany as a Child," in *Huck* (January 27, 2016), https://www.huckmag.com/perspectives/reportage-2/nobel-prize-winning-academic-fled-nazi-germany/ (accessed August 9, 2023).

3   C. Tóibín, *On Elizabeth Bishop* (Princeton: Princeton University Press, 2015), pp. 109-110.

4   A. Hoff, "Owning Memory: Elizabeth Bishop's Authorial Restraint," in *Biography* 31, 4 (2008), pp. 577-594; "An Introduction to Confessional Poetry: How a Newly Personal Mode of Writing Popularized Exploring the Self," *Poetry Foundation* (November 15, 2009), https://www.poetryfoundation.org/collections/151109/an-introduction-to-confessional-poetry (accessed August 9, 2023).

5   T. Faber, *Faber & Faber: The Untold Story* (London: Faber & Faber, 2019), p. 238; J. Mullan, "The History of Faber: 1950s," *Faber Blog* (May 4, 2016), https://www.faber.co.uk/blog/about/faber-1950s/ (accessed December 15, 2021).

6   For a history of this Bendorf-Sayn institution after a December 1940 law segregating Jewish and non-Jewish patients in German hospitals see: Klee, *"Euthanasie" im Dritten Reich*, pp. 277-279.

7   J. Winter, "Our Autofiction Fixation," *New York Times* (March 14, 2021), https://www.nytimes.com/2021/03/14/books/review/autofiction-my-dark-vanessa-american-dirt-the-need-kate-elizabeth-russell-jeanine-cummins-helen-phillips.html (accessed August 9, 2023).

8   H. Pars, *Noch leuchten die Bilder: Schicksale von Meisterwerken der Kunst* (Stuttgart: Europäischer Buchklub, 1957), p. 359.

9   H. Pars, *Pictures in Peril* (London: Faber & Faber, 1957); Landesarchiv Baden-Württemberg/Hauptstaatsarchiv Stuttgart, "Findbuch Q 2/46: Nachlass von Dr. Hans Diebow (1896-1975), Journalist, Zeichner und Schriftsteller," https://www2.landesarchiv-bw.de/ofs21/olf/einfueh.php?bestand=54207 (accessed August 9, 2023); "Schwarz van Berk, Hans (1902-1973)," in *Bundesarchiv, Nachlassdatenbank* (2004/2005), https://www.bundesarchiv.de/nachlassdatenbank/viewsingle.php?person_id=12988&asset_id=14079 (accessed August 9, 2023).

10 Quoted in E. Courtemanche, "Games that Make Nothing Happen: H.G. Wells and the Collapse of Literature," in *Journal of Victorian Literature* 21, 2 (2016), pp. 246-249.

CHAPTER 9

1   The birth described here was an Archers event in 1967. See: K. Davies, "The Archers: Six Diamond Decades – The 1960s," *The Archers Blog* (December 1, 2010), https://www.bbc.co.uk/blogs/thearchers/2010/12/six_diamond_decades_-_the_1960.html (accessed August 23, 2023).

2   Faber, *Faber & Faber*, pp. 164-165; M. Stasio, "P.D. James, Creator of the Adam Dalgliesh Mysteries, Dies at 94," *The New York Times* (November 27, 2014), https://www.nytimes.com/2014/11/28/arts/international/p-d-james-mystery-novelist-known-as-queen-of-crime-dies-at-94.html (accessed August 16, 2023).

3   Faber, *Faber & Faber*, pp. 264-265; p. 275; pp. 292-293.

4   See for these events: S. Bedell Smith, *Prince Charles: The Passions and Paradoxes of an Improbable Life* (New York: Random House, 2017).

5   L. Riefenstahl, *Vanishing Africa* (New York: Harmony, 1982), pp. 18-20; see on Riefenstahl's representations of East Africa: G. Meiu, "Riefenstahl on Safari: Embodied Contemplation in East Africa," *Anthropology Today* 24, 2 (2008), pp. 18-22.

6   See for the life story of Esther Fairfax and her mother Lotte Berk: E. Fairfax, *My Improper Mother and Me* (Hebden Bridge: Pomona, 2010).

7   B. Hicok, *Elizabeth Bishop's Brazil* (Charlottesville: University of Virginia Press, 2016); for the coffee fragment see: A. Quinn (ed.), Elizabeth Bishop, *Edgar Allan Poe & The Juke-Box: Uncollected Poems, Drafts and Fragments* (New York: Farrar, 2006), p. 149.

CHAPTER 10

1   A. Gernhardt and R. Gernhardt, *A Pig That Is Kind Won't Be Left Behind* (London: Jonathan Cape, 1981); Gernhardt/Gernhardt, *Ein gutes Schwein bleibt nicht allein* (Frankfurt am Main: Insel, 1980); Gernhardt/ Gernhardt, *What a Day* (London: Jonathan Cape, 1980); Gernhardt/ Gernhardt, *Was für ein Tag* (Frankfurt am Main: Fischer, 1978).

2   Kathrine Talbot's first published translation from the French: Brigitte Lozerechs *L'intérimaire*. See the critical view on her translation in S. Laschever, "Seeking Respect," *New York Times* (September 16, 1984), p. 41. Talbot then translated short stories by Leonora Carrington (Carrington, *The House of Fear: Notes from Down Below*, New York: E.P. Dutton 1988); see for the praise: R. Burgin, "Paranoia, Surrealism, Madness," *New York Times* (November 27, 1988), p. 29.

3   K. Gershon, *We Came As Children: A Collective Autobiography* (London: Papermac, 1989), pp. 7-9.

4   V. Harrison, "Recording a Life: Elizabeth Bishop's Letters to Ilse and Kit Barker," in *Contemporary Literature* 29, 4 (1988), pp. 498-517. A brief essay on Talbot's poetry did appear in her lifetime: A. Oldham, "Noël Welch and Kathrine Talbot," in *PN Review* 31, 3 (2005): pp. 8-12.

5   Kit Barker reported that he hallucinated a blue tulip after the accident (Fraser, *Chameleon Poet*, p. 77); "The Blue Tulip" is quoted in Fraser, *Chameleon Poet*, p. 78.

6   In these years, however, Kathrine Talbot, the translator, did work for an American anthology collecting source material regarding the Jewish history of Bohemia and Moravia, including documents relating to the Holocaust. See W. Iggers (ed.), *The Jews of Bohemia and Moravia: A Historical Reader* (Detroit: Wayne State University Press, 1992).

7   D. Vincent, "RP or Received Pronunciation – The Characteristically British Accent," in *ELT Learning Journeys* (December 9, 2015), https://eltlearningjourneys.com/2015/12/09/received-pronunciation/ (accessed August 9, 2023).

8   S. Smith and J. Watson, *Reading Autobiography: A Guide for Interpreting Life Narratives* (Minneapolis: University of Minnesota Press, 2010); B. Yagoda, *Memoir: A History* (New York: Riverhead, 2009); M. Erben, "Britain: 20th-Century Auto/biography," in M. Jolly (ed.), *Encyclopedia of Life Writing: Autobiographical and Biographical Forms*, Vol. 1 (London: Fitzroy Dearborn, 2001), pp. 146-148; H. Buss, "Memoirs," in *Enyclopedia of Life Writing*, Vol. 2, pp. 595-597.

9   This (perhaps naïve) take follows Colm Tóibín's approach to Elizabeth Bishop's poetry as "nonfiction" and speculatively reads Talbot's poems in the same mode (Tóibín, *On Elizabeth Bishop*, p. 146). The loose style of her poems, reminiscent of journal entries, might support this interpretation. A collection of her poems was self-published in 1998 and contained some poems that had previously come out in literary magazines: K. Talbot, *Saturday Victory* (Midhurst: IB Press, 1998).

10 M. Hirsch, *Family Frames: Photography, Narrative, and Postmemory* (Cambridge: Harvard University Press, 1997), pp. 22-23; see also later, connecting feminism and "postmemory:" M. Hirsch, *The Generation of Postmemory: Writing and Visual Culture after the Holocaust* (New York: Columbia University Press, 2012), pp. 15-18.

11 M. Schmandt, "Zur Geschichte der Juden in Bingen," in H. Berkessel et al. (eds.), *Leuchte des Exils: Zeugnisse jüdischen Lebens in Mainz und Bingen* (Oppenheim: Nünnerich-Asmus, 2016), pp. 37-39; J. Götten, "Überblick zur Geschichte der Juden in Bingen," in B. Giesbert, B. Götz and J. Götten (eds.), *Juden in Bingen, Beiträge zu ihrer Geschichte* (Bingen: Arbeitskreis Jüdisches Bingen, 2015), pp. 30-35; Bernard, "alles war beschmutzt...".

12 A. Oldham, *Everyone Was Working: Writers and Artists in Postwar* St Ives. (St. Ives: Tate, 2002).

13 In collaboration with her son, Ilse Barker (not Kathrine Talbot) self-published a booklet with a story about a group of Jewish girls from Bingen/Rhine on a hiking tour in the summer of 1935: I. Barker, *Fragments from a Cuttingroom Floor: Recollections of a Walking Tour* (Midhurst: Midhurst and Petworth Printers, 2003).

14 "Howard Kent: Obituary," *The Guardian* (February 24, 2005), https://www.theguardian.com/news/2005/feb/24/guardianobituaries (accessed August 9, 2023).

15 A. Oldham, "Ilse Barker: Obituary," *The Guardian* (June 3, 2006), https://www.theguardian.com/news/2006/jun/03/guardianobituaries. germany (accessed August 23, 2023).

CHAPTER 11

1 "Lausanne," *Feuille d'Avis des Lausanne* (March 9, 1935), p. 12.

2 Having organized much of the future West Germany's monetary reform, Tenenbaum was also known as "the father of the Deutsche Mark." For his biography: A. Rodriguez-Giovo, "Ecolint's Jewish Heritage," (Geneva: Ecolint, 2021) (unpublished); R. Nef and B. Ruetz, "Starkes Stück: Wie der jüdische Offizier Edward A. Tenenbaum vor 60 Jahren den Deutschen zur D-Mark verhalf," *Jüdische Allgemeine* (June 19, 2008), https://www.juedische-allgemeine.de/allgemein/starkes-stueck/ (accessed August 9, 2023).

3 See: Yagoda, *Memoir*; G. Tomson, "More Life: On Contemporary Autofiction and the Scourge of 'Relatability,'" *Michigan Quarterly Review* (August 8, 2018), https://sites.lsa.umich.edu/mqr/2018/08/more-life-on-contemporary-autofiction-and-the-scourge-of-relatability/ (accessed August 16, 2023).

4 On silence and intergenerational trauma: M. Lasker-Wallfisch, *Briefe nach Breslau: Meine Geschichte über drei Generationen* (Berlin: Insel, 2020); C. Kidron, "Breaching the Wall of Traumatic Silence: Holocaust Survivor and Descendant Person-Objects Relations and the Material Transmission of the Genocidal Past," in *Journal of Material Culture* 17, 1 (2012), pp. 3-21.

5 K. Prager, "'Exemplary Lives'? Thoughts on Exile, Gender and Life-Writing," in C. Brinson and A. Hammel (eds.), *Exile and Gender I: Literature and the Press* (Leiden: Brill, 2016), pp. 5-18.

6 W.G. Sebald, *Austerlitz* (2003) (Frankfurt am Main: Fischer, 2006), pp. 325-326. On the marginality of women's voices in the history of German Jewish refugees to Great Britain see: A. Davis, "Belonging and

'Unbelonging:' Jewish Refugee and Survivor Women in 1950s Britain," in *Women's History Review* 26, 1 (2017), pp. 130-146; on Sebald see: A. Oesmann, "Sebald's Melancholic Method: Writing as Ethical Memory in *Austerlitz*," in *Monatshefte* 106, 3 (2014), pp. 452-471 and for critical takes: M. Modlinger, "'You Can't Change Names and Feel the Same:' The Kindertransport Experience of Susi Bechhöfer in W.G. Sebald's *Austerlitz*," in A. Hammel and B. Lewkowicz (eds.), *The Kindertransport to Britain 1938/39: New Perspectives* (Leiden: Brill, 2012), pp. 219-232, and C. Angier, *Speak, Silence: In Search of W.G. Sebald* (London: Bloomsbury, 2021).

7   S. Friedländer, *Das Dritte Reich und die Juden: Die Jahre der Verfolgung, 1933-1939* (Munich: Beck, 2000), p. 308.

8   Elise Bath (The Wiener Holocaust Library), "ITS Report: The Groß Family" (2021) (e-mailed to the author, April 9, 2021) (information drawn from digital copy of the International Tracing Service archive, physical copy in Arolsen Archive, Germany); "2. Deportation am 30. April 1942," Mahnmal Koblenz (2021), https://web25.otto.kundenserver42.de/Mahnmal_NEU/index.php/daten-und-fakten/deportationen-von-juden-aus-koblenz-und-umgebung/555-juden-aus-dem-landkreis-koblenz-die-am-30-04-1942-abtransportiert-worden-sind (accessed August 9, 2023); S. Hänschen, *Das Transitghetto Izbica im System des Holocaust* (Berlin: Metropol, 2018), pp. 286-292.

9   A. Hájková, *The Last Ghetto: An Everyday History of Theresienstadt* (New York: Oxford University Press, 2020), pp. 100-131.

10   E. Bath, "ITS Report;" "Transport Ep from Theresienstadt, Ghetto, Czechoslovakia to Auschwitz Birkenau, Extermination Camp, Poland on 09/10/1944," Yad Vashem: The World Holocaust Remembrance Center, https://deportation.yadvashem.org/index.html?language=en&itemId=5092066 (accessed August 9, 2023).

Bibliography

Allen, W. "Henry Green," in *Penguin New Writing* (London: Penguin, 1945), pp. 144-155.

Angier, C. *Speak, Silence: In Search of W.G. Sebald* (London: Bloomsbury, 2021).

Barker, C. *The Arms of the Infinite: Elizabeth Smart and George Barker* (Hebden Bridge: Pomona, 2006).

Barker, I. *Fragments from a Cutting Room Floor: Recollections of a Walking Tour* (Midhurst: Midhurst and Petworth Printers, n.d.).

Bernard, B. "'...alles war beschmutzt und besudelt:' Das Judenpogrom in Bingen und die Zerstörung der Binger Synagogen am 10. November 1938," in M. Schmandt (ed.), *Bingen im Nationalsozialismus: Quellen und Studien* (Bad Kreuznach: Matthias Ess, 2018), pp. 303-359.

Bernard, B. "Tourismus in Bingen in den 1930er Jahren," in M. Schmandt (ed.), *Bingen im Nationalsozialismus: Quellen und Studien* (Bad Kreuznach: Matthias Ess, 2018), pp. 211-261.

Bihler, L. *Cities of Refuge: German Jews in London and New York, 1935-1945* (Albany: State University of New York Press, 2019).

Bishop, E., *Edgar Allan Poe & the Juke-Box: Uncollected Poems, Drafts and Fragments* (New York: Farrar, 2006).

Black, E. *IBM and the Holocaust: The Strategic Alliance between Nazi Germany and America's Most Powerful Corporation* (New York: Dialog, 2012).

Boggess, C. *James Still: A Life* (Lexington: University Press of Kentucky, 2017).

Bollauf, T. *Dienstmädchen-Emigration: Die Flucht jüdischer Frauen aus Österreich und Deutschland nach England 1938/39* (Vienna: LIT, 2011).

Braslow, J. *Mental Ills and Bodily Cures: Psychiatric Treatment in the First Half of the Twentieth Century* (Berkeley: University of California Press, 1997).

Brennan, M. *Modernism's Masculine Subjects: Matisse, The New York School, and Post-Painterly Abstraction* (Cambridge: MIT Press, 2004).

Brinson, C. "A Woman's Place...? German-Speaking Women in Exile in Britain, 1933-1945," in *German Life and Letters*, 51, 2 (April 1998), pp. 204-224.

Brinson, C. "Introduction," in R. Borchard (ed.), *We Are Strangers Here: An 'Enemy Alien' in Prison in 1940* (London: Vallentine Mitchell, 2008), pp. 1-15.

Brittain, V. *Seed of Chaos: What Mass Bombing Really Means* (London: New Vision, 1944).

Brunnhuber, N. *The Faces of Janus: English-Language Fiction by German-Speaking Exiles in Great Britain, 1933-45* (Oxford: Peter Lang, 2005).

Bublitz, S. *The World of Rosamunde Pilcher* (New York: St. Martin's, 1996).

Buss, H. "Memoirs," in M. Jolly (ed.), *Encyclopedia of Life Writing: Autobiographical and Biographical Forms*, Vol. 2 (London: Fitzroy Dearborn, 2001), pp. 595-597.

Cesarani, D. "Great Britain," in D. Wyman and C. Rosenzweig (eds.), *The World Reacts to the Holocaust* (Baltimore: Johns Hopkins University Press, 1996), pp. 599-641.

Cesarani, D. and Sundquist, E. *After the Holocaust: Challenging the Myth of Silence* (London: Routledge, 2012).

Chappell, C. *Island of Barbed Wire: Internment on the Isle of Man in World War Two* (London: Robert Hale, 1984).

Courtemanche, E. "Games that Make Nothing Happen: H.G. Wells and the Collapse of Literature," in *Journal of Victorian Literature*, 21, 2 (2016), pp. 246-249.

Craig-Norton, J. "Refugees at the Margins: Jewish Domestics in Britain, 1938-1945," in *Shofar*, 37, 3 (2019), pp. 295-330.

Davis, A. "Belonging and 'Unbelonging:' Jewish Refugee and Survivor Women in 1950s Britain," in *Women's History Review*, 26, 1 (2017), pp. 130-146.

Diamant, K. *Kafka's Last Love: The Mystery of Dora Diamant* (London: Secker & Warburg, 2003).

Erben, M. "Britain: 20th-Century Auto/biography," in M. Jolly (ed.), *Encyclopedia of Life Writing: Autobiographical and Biographical Forms*, Vol. 1 (London: Fitzroy Dearborn, 2001), pp. 146-148.

Faber, T. *Faber & Faber: The Untold Story.* (London: Faber & Faber, 2019).

Fairfax, E. *My Improper Mother and Me* (Hebden Bridge: Pomona, 2010).

Ford, F. *The March of Literature: Confucius to Modern Times* (London: Allen & Unwin, 1947).

Fraser, R. *The Chameleon Poet: A Life of George Barker* (London: Jonathan Cape, 2001).

Friedlander, K. *The Psycho-Analytical Approach to Juvenile Delinquency: Theory, Case-Studies, Treatment* (London: Kegan Paul, Trench, Trubner, 1947).

Friedländer, S. *Das Dritte Reich und die Juden: Die Jahre der Verfolgung, 1933-1939* (München: Beck, 2000).

Gabriel, M. *Ninth Street Women: Lee Krasner, Elaine De Kooning, Grace Hartigan, Joan Mitchell, and Helen Frankenthaler: Five Painters and the Movement that Changed Modern Art* (New York: Little Brown, 2018).

Gardiner, J. *Wartime: Britain 1939-1945* (London: Headline, 2004).

Gershon, K. *We Came As Children: A Collective Autobiography* (London: Papermac, 1989).

Goldberg, K. "Wie der Wein in Mitteleuropa jüdisch wurde," in A. Lehnardt (ed.), *Wein und Judentum* (Berlin: Neofelis, 2014), pp. 229-246.

Göpfert, R. *Der jüdische Kindertransport von Deutschland nach England 1938/39: Geschichte und Erinnerung* (Frankfurt am Main: Campus, 1999).

Grahame, K. *The Wind in the Willows* (London: Hamlyn, 1989).

Green, H. *Loving* (London: Harvill, 1992).

Greenland, C. "At the Crichton Royal with William Mayer-Gross," in *History of Psychiatry* 13 (2002), pp. 467-474.

Gross, W. "Zur Phänomenologie abnormer Glücksgefühle," in *Zeitschrift für Pathopsychologie* 2 (1914), pp. 588-610.

Hájková, A. *The Last Ghetto: An Everyday History of Theresienstadt* (New York: Oxford University Press, 2020).

Hänschen, S. *Das Transitghetto Izbica im System des Holocaust* (Berlin: Metropol, 2018)

Harrison, V. "Recording a Life: Elizabeth Bishop's Letters to Ilse and Kit Barker," in *Contemporary Literature*, 29, 4 (1988), pp. 498-517.

Herbert, G. "The Affliction (I)," in H. Wilcox (ed.), *The English Poems of George Herbert* (Cambridge: Cambridge UP, 2007), pp. 162-3.

Hewison, R. *Under Siege: Literary Life in London 1939-1945* (London: Weidenfeld and Nicolson, 1977).

Hicok, B. *Elizabeth Bishop's Brazil* (Charlottesville: University of Virginia Press, 2016).

Hirsch, M. *Family Frames: Photography, Narrative, and Postmemory* (Cambridge: Harvard University Press, 1997).

Hirsch, M. *The Generation of Postmemory: Writing and Visual Culture after the Holocaust* (New York: Columbia University Press, 2012), pp. 15-18.

Huxley, A. *Ends and Means: An Enquiry into the Nature of Ideals and into the Methods Employed for their Realization* (London: Chatto & Windus, 1980).

James, H. "The Art of Fiction," in L. Edel (ed.), *Henry James: Major Stories and Essays* (New York: Library of America, 1999), pp. 572-593.

James, H. *The Sacred Fount* (New York: Grove, 1979).

Kidron, C. "Breaching the Wall of Traumatic Silence: Holocaust Survivor and Descendant Person-Objects Relations and the Material Transmission of the Genocidal Past," in *Journal of Material Culture*, 17, 1 (2012), pp. 3-21.

Klee, E. *Euthanasie im Dritten Reich: Die Vernichtung lebensunwerten Lebens* (Frankfurt am Main: Fischer, 2014).

Kochan, M. "Women's Experience of Internment," in D. Cesarani and T. Kushner (eds), *The Internment of Aliens in Twentieth Century Britain* (London: Frank Cass, 1993), pp. 147-188.

Kushner, T. "An Alien Occupation: Jewish Refugees and Domestic Service in Britain, 1933-1948," in W. Mosse (ed.), *Second Chance: Two Centuries of German-Speaking Jews in the United Kingdom* (Tübingen: Mohr, 1991), pp. 553-578.

Kushner, T. *The Holocaust and the Liberal Imagination: A Social and Cultural History* (Oxford: Blackwell, 1994).

Kushner, T. "Anti-Semitism and Austerity: The August 1947 Riots in Britain," in P. Panayi (ed.), *Racial Violence in Britain, 1840-1950* (London: Leicester University Press, 1996), pp. 150-170.

Kushner, T. "From 'This Belsen Business' to 'Shoah Business:' History, Memory, and Heritage, 1945-2005," in S. Bardgett and D. Cesarani (eds.), *Belsen 1945: New Historical Perspectives* (London: Vallentine Mitchell, 2006), pp. 189-216.

Kushner, T. "The Holocaust in the British Imagination: The Official Mind and Beyond, 1945 to the Present," in *Holocaust Studies*, 23, 3 (2017), pp. 1-21.

Kynaston, D. *Austerity Britain 1945-1951* (London: Bloomsbury, 2007).

Laurent, L. *A Tale of Internment* (London: Allen & Unwin, 1942).

Lawson, T. and Pearce, A. (eds), *The Palgrave Handbook of Britain and the Holocaust* (London: Palgrave Macmillan, 2020).

Lupton, C. *Reading and the Making of Time in the Eighteenth Century* (Baltimore: Johns Hopkins University Press, 2018).

McDonald, C. "'We Became British Aliens:' Kindertransport Refugees Narrating the Discovery of Their Parents' Fates," in *Holocaust Studies*, 24, 4 (2018), pp. 395-417.

McGurl, M. *The Program Era: Postwar Fiction and the Rise of Creative Writing* (Cambridge: Harvard University Press, 2009).

Meiu, G. "Riefenstahl on Safari: Embodied Contemplation in East Africa," in *Anthropology Today*, 24, 2 (2008), pp. 18-22.

Michaelis-Jena, R. *Auch wir waren des Kaisers Kinder: Lebenserinnerungen* (Lemgo: Wagener, 1985).

Modlinger, M. "You Can't Change Names and Feel the Same: The Kindertransport Experience of Susi Bechhöfer in W.G. Sebald's *Austerlitz*," in A. Hammel and B. Lewkowicz (eds.), *The Kindertransport to Britain 1938/39: New Perspectives* (Leiden: Brill, 2012), pp. 219-232.

Moule, D. *Friend or Foe? The Fascinating Story of Women's Internment during WW II in Port Erin & Port St. Mary, Isle of Man* (Douglas: Rushen Heritage Trust, 2018).

Nesbit, E. *The Wouldbegoods: Being the Further Adventures of the Treasure Seekers* (Harmondsworth: Penguin, 1971).

Neubauer, H. *Black Star: 60 Years of Photojournalism* (Cologne: Könemann, 1997).

Oesmann, A. "Sebald's Melancholic Method: Writing as Ethical Memory in *Austerlitz*," in *Monatshefte*, 106, 3 (2014), pp. 452-471.

Oldham, A. *Everyone Was Working: Writers and Artists in Postwar St. Ives* (St. Ives: Tate, 2002).

Oldham, A. "Noël Welch and Kathrine Talbot," in *PN Review*, 31, 3 (2005), pp. 8-12.

Prager, K. "'Exemplary Lives?' Thoughts on Exile, Gender and Life-Writing," in C. Brinson and A. Hammel (ed.), *Exile and Gender I: Literature and the Press* (Leiden: Brill, 2016), pp. 5-18.

Rempel, R. "The Dilemmas of British Pacifists During World War II," in *The Journal of Modern History*, 50, 4 (1978), pp. D1213-D1229.

Ritchie, J. "German Refugees from Nazism," in P. Panayi (ed.), *Germans in Britain Since 1500* (London: Bloomsbury, 1996), pp. 147-170.

Robinson, A. *The Bleak Midwinter 1947* (Manchester: Manchester University Press, 1987).

Rodenberg, H. *The Making of Ernest Hemingway: Celebrity, Photojournalism, and the Emergence of the Modern Lifestyle Media* (Münster: LIT, 2014).

Schmandt, M. "Zur Geschichte der Juden in Bingen," in H. Berkessel et al. (ed.), *Leuchte des Exils: Zeugnisse jüdischen Lebens in Mainz und Bingen* (Oppenheim: Nünnerich-Asmus, 2016), pp. 37-39.

Segal, L. *Other People's Houses* (London: Sort Of Books, 2018).

Seyfert, M. *Im Niemandsland: Deutsche Exilliteratur in britischer Internierung: Ein unbekanntes Kapitel der Kulturgeschichte des Zweiten Weltkriegs* (Berlin: Arsenal, 1984).

Smart, E. *By Grand Central Station I Sat Down and Wept* (London: Fourth Estate, 2015).

Smith, S. and Watson, J. *Reading Autobiography: A Guide for Interpreting Life Narratives* (Minneapolis: University of Minnesota Press, 2010).

Smith, S.B. *Prince Charles: The Passions and Paradoxes of an Improbable Life* (New York: Random House, 2017).

Später, J. *Siegfried Kracauer: Eine Biographie* (Berlin: Suhrkamp, 2016)

Stopes, M. *Married Love or Love in Marriage* (Oxford: Oxford University Press, 2004).

Strickhausen, W. "Großbritannien," in D. Krohn (eds), *Handbuch der deutschsprachigen Emigration, 1933-1945* (Darmstadt: Wissenschaftliche Buchgesellschaft, 2012), pp. 251-270.

Sullivan, R. *By Heart: Elizabeth Smart. A Life* (New York: Viking, 1991).

Talbot, K. *Fire in the Sun* (New York: Putnam, 1952).

Talbot, K. *The Innermost Cage* (New York: Putnam, 1955).

Talbot, K. *Return* (London: Faber & Faber, 1959).

Talbot, K. *Kit Barker Cornwall 1947-1948: Recollections of Painters and Writers* (St. Ives: Book Gallery, 1993).

Talbot, K. *Saturday Victory* (Midhurst: IB Press, 1998).

Tanner, T. "Introduction," in T. Tanner (ed.), *Henry James* (London: MacMillan, 1968), pp. 11-41.

Tóibín, C. *On Elizabeth Bishop* (Princeton: Princeton University Press, 2015).

Uhlman, F. *The Making of an Englishman* (London: Victor Gollancz, 1960).

Utsch, S. *Sprachwechsel im Exil: Die "linguistische Metamorphose" von Klaus Mann* (Cologne: Böhlau, 2007).

Vietor-Engländer, D. "What's in a Name? What Is Jewishness? New Definitions for Two Generations: Elsa Bernstein, Anna Gmeyner, Ruth Ewald, and Others," in M. Gelber, J. Hessing and R. Jütte (eds.), *Integration und Ausgrenzung: Studien zur deutsch-jüdischen Literatur- und Kulturgeschichte* (Tübingen: Max Niemeyer, 2009), pp. 467-481.

Viney, G. *The Last Hurrah: The 1947 Royal Tour of Southern Africa and the End of Empire* (London: Robinson, 2019).

Wallfisch, M. *Briefe nach Breslau: Meine Geschichte über drei Generationen* (Berlin: Insel, 2020).

White, J. *London in the Twentieth Century: A City and Its People* (London: Vintage, 2001).

Woolf, V. *A Room of One's Own* (London: Hogarth, 1929).

Yagoda, B. *Memoir: A History* (New York: Riverhead, 2009).